```
                                        792
                                        M122
              McCALLUM

       Fun with stagecraft


       DO NOT REMOVE BOOK CARD OR
       DATE DUE SLIP, 15¢ CHARGE FOR
       LOSS OR DAMAGE TO EITHER.


       New Albany - Floyd County Public Library
                New Albany, Indiana
```

FUN WITH STAGECRAFT

by
Andrew McCallum

ENSLOW PUBLISHERS
Bloy Street and Ramsey Avenue
Box 777
Hillside, New Jersey 07205

Line drawings by E. J. O'Toole.

First American Edition 1982.

Copyright © Kaye & Ward Ltd 1977.

All rights reserved.

No part of this book may be reproduced by any means without the written permission of the publisher.

Library of Congress Cataloging in Publication Data:

McCallum, Andrew.
    Fun with stagecraft.

    Includes index.
    1. Stage management.   I. Title.
PN2085.M28   792'.02   80-27686

ISBN 0-89490-008-0

Printed in the United States of America

Contents

Foreword 4
Introduction 5
History of the Stage 7

Modern Stages 15

Scenery—Design and Building 25

Furniture and Props 43

Stage Lighting 53

Sound Effects 69

Makeup, Costume and Wardrobe 77

Backstage Organization 85

Index 93

Foreword

This book introduces the layman to the language and craft of the theater. The terminology of the theater is universal: it can be understood in the wings of theaters from Broadway to Sydney and to the West End of London.

Every group of human beings that congregates must feel the desire to "make theater." When starting out, the simplest things suffice: a bed sheet, old cartons and trunks, the fading dress-ups from Halloweens ago. But for the real enthusiast, the call will be stronger and the demands greater.

In theater, there are no secrets, no mysteries for the initiated only. There are the tried-and-true practices that have been devised by skilled practitioners over the years. Workability, aesthetic satisfaction, and safety are the most important elements in turning make-believe into theater. This fine book contains all the basic information necessary for those who wish to create a theatrical production, whether for a school, college, or amateur player group.

> Nagle Jackson
> Artistic Director
> McCarter Theatre Company
> Princeton, New Jersey

Introduction

When a play is being performed on the stage, it is not only the actors who are working, although they may be the only ones seen and heard by the audience. Behind the scenes, somewhere, is a team of people or a *stage crew* as it is called, that has helped to get the play ready for its performance, and that does all the necessary practical tasks when the play is eventually being performed. These practical tasks will probably include the building and putting up of scenery, the making and use of props, sound and lighting effects, and sometimes even the cleaning of the stage! The importance of good stagecraft is that it helps the actor to give a more convincing performance, thereby increasing the enjoyment of the audience. Backstage work must always be in keeping with the mood and atmosphere of the play being performed, and should be carried out as accurately and as thoroughly as possible, bearing in mind how it will all seem from the audience's point of view. Poor stagecraft, shoddily done, can break the atmosphere of a play and ruin a good performance, but if care and thought have been used, it can be very exciting to be in a team which has contributed to a successful production.

This book will help you to get a lot of fun out of stagecraft and teach you some of the skills necessary to get a play to "sit" comfortably on a stage.

HISTORY OF THE STAGE

Before you begin to learn about stagecraft, it is essential that you know something about the different types of stages which you may come across. The history of the theater stretches over many thousands of years, so it would be useful for us to look briefly at some of the ancestors of the modern stage.

Illustration 1 is a well-preserved example of a theater used by the ancient Greeks, built about four hundred years before the birth of Christ. The *auditorium* (where the audience sat) was semicircular, and the circular stage was at ground level. Behind the stage was a wall, with doors to provide entrances for the actors, and leading to dressing rooms and storage areas. This rear wall, which was very high and part of the backstage building, provided a background to the action. The theater was open-air and there were no curtains screening the actors from the audience. It is significant that a theater of such simple design enabled everyone in the auditorium to have a perfect view of the stage and to hear clearly, even when the actors talked quietly.

In England, in the year 1425 A.D., a play was performed called *The Castle of Perseverance.* Illustration 2 is a drawing of the "scenery design." As you can see there is no conventional stage and auditorium, but several raised platforms in a circle, with another platform (the castle) in the center. The audience was able to view the action from any angle it pleased, and move around while it watched. At this time it was usual for the theater to move about, and a play could be performed anywhere providing there was a raised stage and a group of people to watch. In those towns which had a yearly play festival, plays would be performed from the tops of carts, which could be pulled from one place to another, wherever an audience had gathered. The theater literally went to the people! The audience was able to see and hear clearly and therefore able

1. The ancient Greek theater at Epidaurus, showing part of the semicircular auditorium rising above the stage. The buildings at the back of the stage have long since disappeared. —*Camera and Pen International.*

History of the Stage   9

to become completely involved with the play, which is the most basic requirement of good stagecraft.

Illustration 3 is a drawing of the type of theater popular in London during and just after the reign of Queen Elizabeth I. The stage thrusts out into the auditorium and the audience sat or stood round the three sides, or in the tiers of balconies which were let into the circular wall that enclosed the whole theater. At the back of the main stage was a small inner stage which could be curtained off. The two doors on either side led to workshops, dressing rooms, and storage areas. The first balcony above the inner stage was useful as an acting area on a higher level, and the second balcony held the musicians who supplied incidental music. Gods and other supernatural characters could be suspended by a rope and flown from this balcony. The stages were often equipped with trap doors to allow witches and spirits to appear and disappear.

2. *The Castle of Perseverance.*

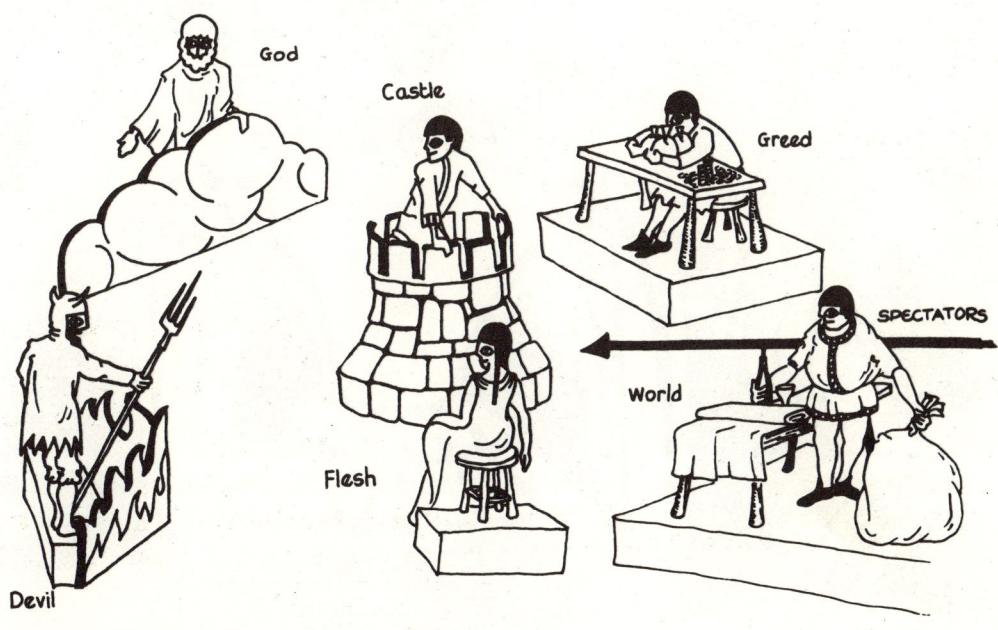

4. The stage of the Royalty Theatre, London, 1815.

3. *Opposite:* An Elizabethan playhouse.

The stages we have discussed so far used little or no scenery, as the audience was required to imagine a scene rather than actually see it, but by the middle of the seventeenth century styles had changed so much that the onlookers demanded to have everything depicted on the stage as realistically as possible. Illustration 4 shows how this demand brought about a complete change in theater design. The stage no longer thrust into the auditorium but became enclosed by a massive gilt picture frame called the *proscenium arch*. Heavy curtains could be let down from the top, or drawn from the sides of the proscenium, screening the stage from the audience while the elaborately realistic scenery was being changed. Theaters now had roofs to them, and the stage was lit by burning candles. Subsequently gas was used, and eventually electricity.

From the auditorium, the stage now looked like a closed-in picture, but it is obvious that some of the audience in the front balconies had difficulty in seeing all of that picture!

5. Model of a Greek theater.   *—David Richardson, reproduced by permission of Mr. J.K. Wilkinson.*

History of the Stage

It is interesting to compare the different designs of theaters and stages as they developed over the years. All of them have influenced the types of stages most widely used today.

If you enjoy making models, try making one based on one of the theaters illustrated in this chapter. Strong cardboard and styrofoam are useful materials to use. Your local library or a museum may have other pictures of stages, and if you are lucky enough to have a theater near where you live, you would probably be able to get permission to visit it and look around the stage. You can then decide which of the styles you have learned about influenced its design.

MODERN STAGES

The different types of stages in use today have developed from a mixture of the designs described in the first chapter. Although there are many variations, modern stages fall generally into three categories:

        the proscenium arch stage
        the theater-in-the-round stage
        the arena stage

    The arena stage, of which illustration 6 is an example, is the most flexible and the easiest to work on. Scenery is not required, although a little can be used as long as it does not obstruct the audience's view. Storage areas for costume and props are behind the rear wall, while the lighting-control and sound-effects equipment are usually positioned in the front of the theater behind the audience—the *front of house* as it is called.

    The stage for theater-in-the-round (illustration 7) is also quite flexible and easy to work on, as long as you remember that the audience is on all sides, preventing the use of scenery or furniture higher than the front row. Areas for the stage crew have to be hidden behind the audience, which is where the sound effects and lighting controls are placed.

6. New Jersey Shakespeare Festival. —*Photograph by Blair Holley.*

7. The Victoria Theatre, England. —*Photograph by Richard Smiles.*

The proscenium arch stage (illustration 8) is traditionally the most popular type. A real, though two-dimensional picture can be created on it, but it requires more planning and work for the stage crew than the others.

8. McCarter Theatre production of *A Christmas Carol*.
—*Photograph by Robert I. Faulkner.*

MAKING A GROUND PLAN AND SIGHT LINES

When it has been decided which play is to be rehearsed, and the cast has been chosen, your first job is to make a ground plan of the stage on which you will be working. Illustration 9 is an example and shows a ground plan of a proscenium arch stage which is, as you can see, a view of the stage looking directly downwards. To make such a plan you will need:

>a pencil
>a pen (preferably felt tipped)
>a ruler
>a long tape measure
>graph paper

The *cyclorama* (which we shortenen to "cyc" for greater convenience) is the name given to the concave sheet of canvas suspended at the rear of the stage, on which colored lighting can be projected. On amateur stages this is usually a flat wall painted white. The *traverse curtains* are situated midway between the cyc and the front curtains on the proscenium arch. They can be pulled together to allow another scene to be set up behind while one is playing in front of them. Not all stages have these curtains. *Legs* are either *flats* (flat pieces of scenery) painted black or white, or narrow curtains slightly higher than the proscenium, which protrude from the *wings* and mask or hide the back of the stage from the audience. The ground plan shown has only four legs, but to mask effectively on a deeper stage more may be required. The *apron* or forestage is that part which projects out from the front curtains. To indicate which side of the stage is being referred to you can say stage left or right (S.L. or S.R.), but remember that it is the actor's left and right as he faces the auditorium, NOT the audience's. Similarly the area of the stage towards the apron is known as *downstage* and the area towards the cyc is *upstage.*

To make your plan, with the long tape measure, take the

following measurements of the stage area:
> distance from the cyc to traverse curtains (if any)
> distance from the cyc to front curtains
> distance from the cyc to edge of apron

Then take the width of the proscenium arch and finally the width of the apron.

Now transfer the dimensions to the graph paper, suitably scaling them down to fit before making your drawing. The scale you choose depends not only on the size of the paper but on the size of the stage. Try and make the scale as large as possible—one large square to equal one foot is ideal. Begin by drawing a straight line about one square in from the top edge of the paper. This will represent the cyc and can be used as a basis from which to measure and mark in the curtain line, traverse line, and edge of the apron. Try and place the whole plan centrally on the paper, don't squash it into the sides. When you have pencilled in all the necessary lines, go over them in pen, using straight lines for the cyc, proscenium opening, and the apron, and wavy lines for the curtains. Now find the exact center of the cyc and draw a *center line* from the cyc to the apron. This will be useful when working out the position of scenery, as all eyes in the audience are naturally focused on the center of the stage. Label the plan in small writing, adding the name of the stage you have used, together with the scale. The plan is now complete, except for the sight lines (marked S.L. in illustration 9).

Sight lines help to ensure that there are no areas of the stage which will be hidden from view. To decide where the sight lines are on your stage you will need the help of a friend with a chair. Place the chair on the extreme left or right of the front row where the audience will be sitting. Your friend must then sit in the chair and face the stage. Place the tape measure against the cyc, on the ground, starting directly in line with the edge of the proscenium—position "A" in illustration 10. Begin walking slowly towards the center of the stage, keeping close to the cyc,

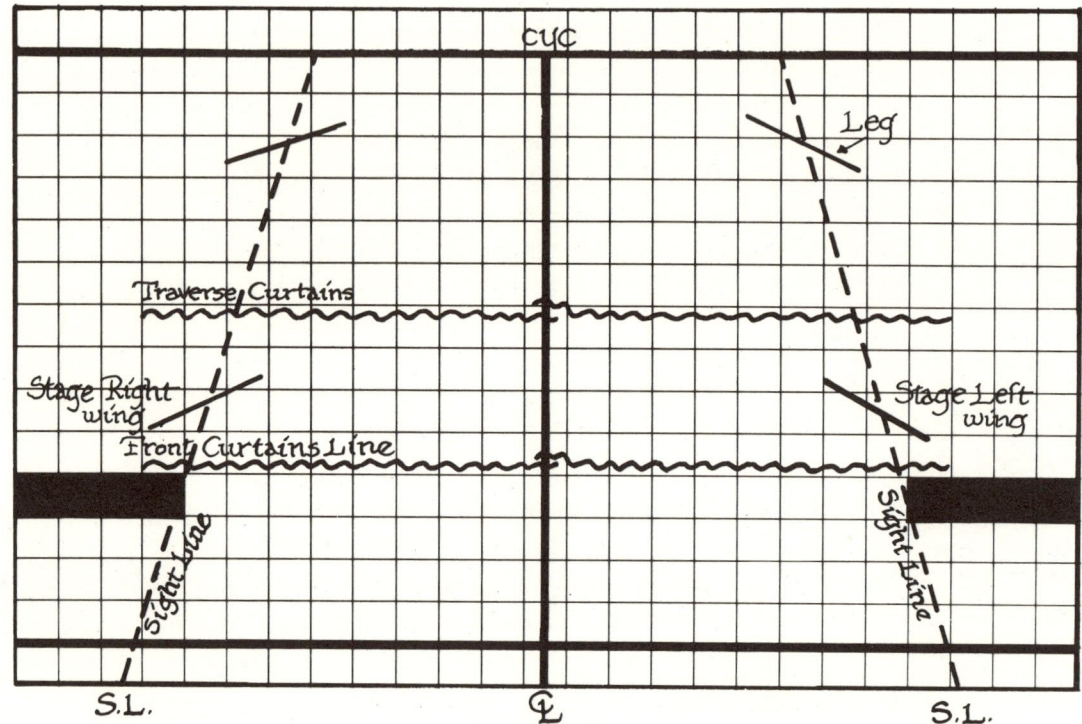

9. Ground plan of a proscenium arch stage. All p.a. stages are similar to this in design, although dimensions—width of stage, depth of stage, area of apron, etc.—can vary enormously. —*S. MacGregor.*

and as soon as your friend sees you, he must shout "stop." This is position "B" in the diagram, and is the beginning of the sight line. Make a note of the distance. Now repeat the procedure on the other side of the stage. Your friend will have to move to the other end of the front row. On your ground plan draw a dotted line from position "B" extending out over the apron and just touching the corner of each proscenium pillar. You now have an exact idea of which areas of the stage will be in full view of all the members of the audience, no matter where they sit. Any scenery, such as walls, doors, or windows will have to be set on

Modern Stages 21

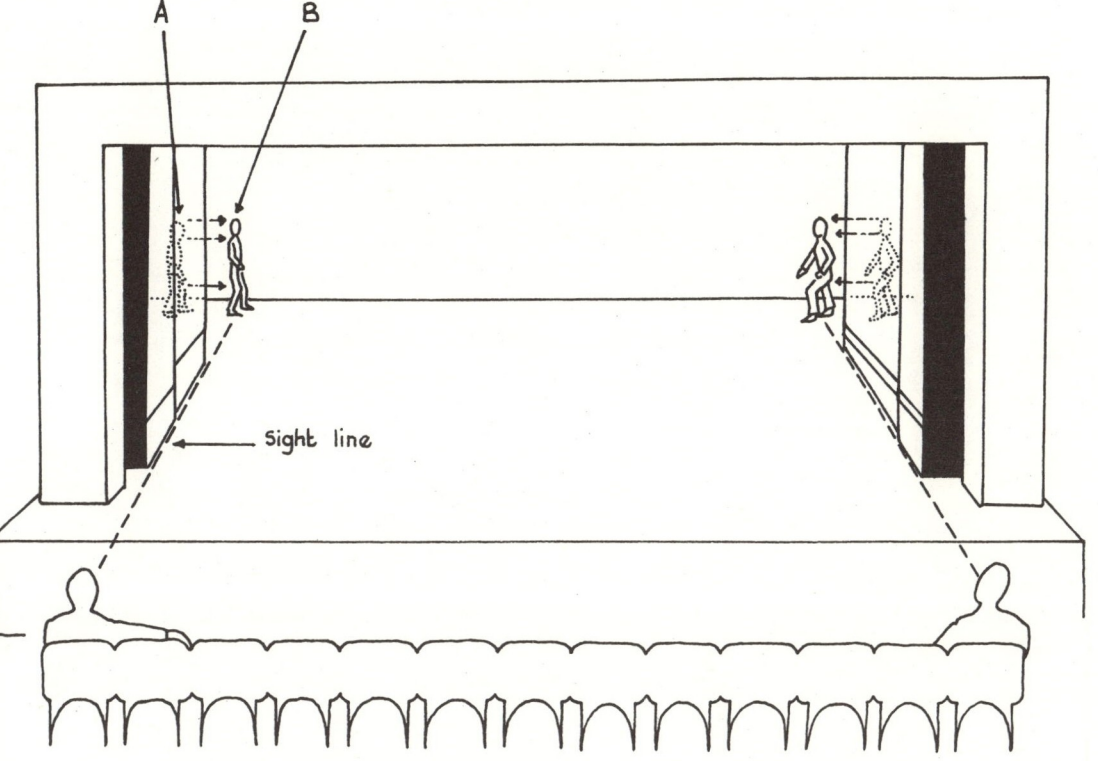

10. How to determine horizontal sight lines.

the sight lines or even further out if you wish, but no further in towards the wings. For stages with very narrow wings, the extra space created by the sight lines can be extremely useful.

This takes care of the view from the auditorium looking *horizontally,* but remember that people will look UP from their chairs, and if they are in a balcony will look DOWN on the stage, so you must take into account a *vertical* sight line. All that is needed is the height of the proscenium opening, and this should be written in on your plan in its actual height, not to scale.

Scenery must then be constructed about one foot higher than the proscenium, so that the tops of the flats extend behind the *borders,* which is the name given to the series of narrow curtains running above the stage from wing to wing. If this is not done there may be an embarrassing gap between the top of a flat and the lower edge of a border! (Illustration 11.)

For arena and in-the-round stages ground plans are made in the same way but are easier to construct. There are no wings, curtains, or aprons. These plans should have a line to indicate where the front row of the audience is to be placed, which will be semicircular for an arena stage, and straight lines making a square or rectangle for in-the-round. The lines should be broken where entrances are to be placed. On these stages the only important sight lines are the vertical ones. Ideally the seating should slant up from the level of the stage, so that everyone

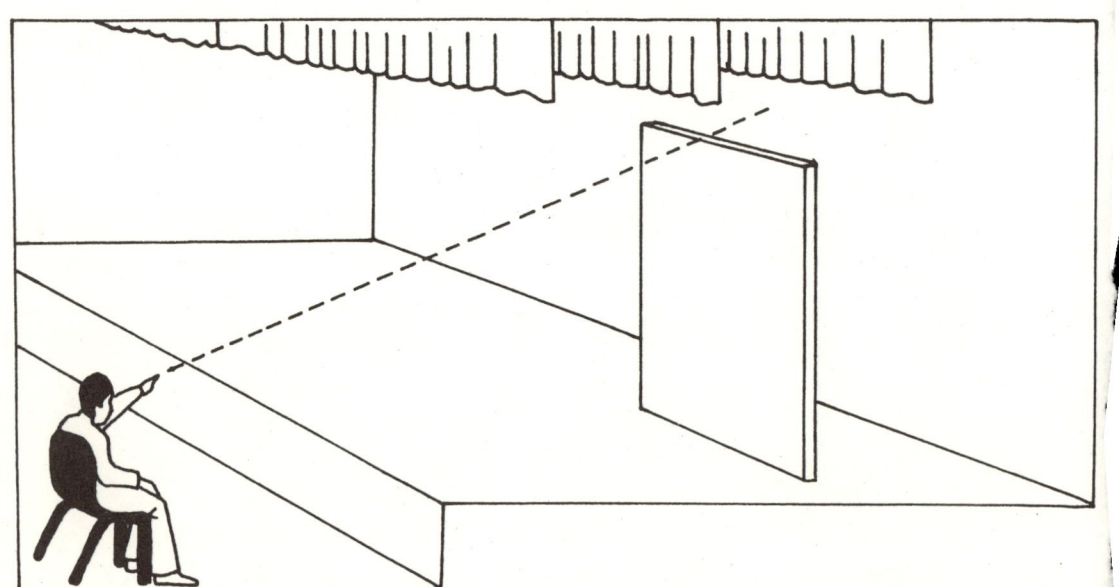

11. Vertical sight line showing that the flats are too short.

Modern Stages

behind the front row has a clear view of the stage and not of the heads in front of them.

Proscenium arch stage positions apply to arena, but in-the-round naturally has no up, down, left, or right. The ground plan for this stage is best marked with two center lines that cross. From these, the positions of furniture can be marked accurately on the plan when needed.

Ask for permission to make a ground plan of a stage accessible to you. Make it carefully to scale, and if it is a proscenium put in the sight lines and lable it. The only dimension to put on the plan is the height of the proscenium opening, or for an arena stage, the height of the rear wall. Remember to show the scale you have used.

This section has been concerned only with three basic types of stage, but there are others such as the *thrust* stage which is not unlike the Elizabethan stage shown in the previous section. But a stage is an acting area which can be anywhere—on the floor in a corner of a large room or in the middle of a field— so long as there is room for an audience to see clearly.

SCENERY–DESIGN AND BUILDING

Scenery is used on the stage to mask the wings and backstage areas with a picture which is both enjoyable to look at and entirely in keeping with the atmosphere and mood of the play. This is most important because good scenery can enhance the actors' performances and increase the enjoyment of the audience. The design of the *set*—which is the total amount of the scenery used for each act—is usually the producer's job, as he is ultimately responsible for choosing everything that the audience will see. Often the same set is used throughout a play.

Set design begins only after a thorough knowledge of the play has been gained and the playwright's stage directions have been read and understood also. The shape and coloring of the set will be determined by an understanding of the mood of the play, together with considerations of the size of the cast and whereabouts they will need to enter and exit. Small doorways are impractical if large props have to be brought on, or flamboyant costumes are worn, making the wearer wider in figure than normal! Large crowds will need plenty of room to get on and off, and should not be restricted by a stage cluttered with furniture and scenery. All these are necessary

12. Set design for *Rookery Nook* by Ben Travers.

considerations, and the designing of a set is basic to the planning of the whole show.

On pages 26, 27, and 28 are two pictures of set designs with their ground plans. Illustration 12 is a design for a farce called *Rookery Nook*. This is a realistic set, because the scenery creates a "real" picture of a hallway inside a cottage. Like all realistic sets it has the appearance of a room with the fourth wall removed to allow us to see the action. Because the stage is enclosed we call this a *box* set. Outside the window is a garden which can be seen when the front door is opened. When the other doors are opened they reveal part of the room behind them. The ground plan (illustration 13) shows you how this is done. Behind the windows and doors are masking flats, suitably

Scenery—Design and Building

painted and carefully positioned. Notice on the ground plan there are arrows to indicate which way the doors are to open. If you stand in the hall of your own house and open the door, you can check that this arrangement is correct.

Illustration 15 makes no attempt to represent a real picture. It is virtually *abstract* allowing the same set to be used for different scenes without having to *strike* (dismantle) one scene and *set up* a new one. This is a necessary economy, as frequent scene changes can be expensive as well as time-wasting. The set in illustration 12 also remains unchanged throughout the play. Illustration 14 is designed for the Gilbert and Sullivan opera *The Yeomen of the Guard,* where the action takes place in the Tower of London. The story is tragic. The platforms, painted in black, give an effect of grandeur and solid grimness, providing a dramatically contrasting background for the large cast and

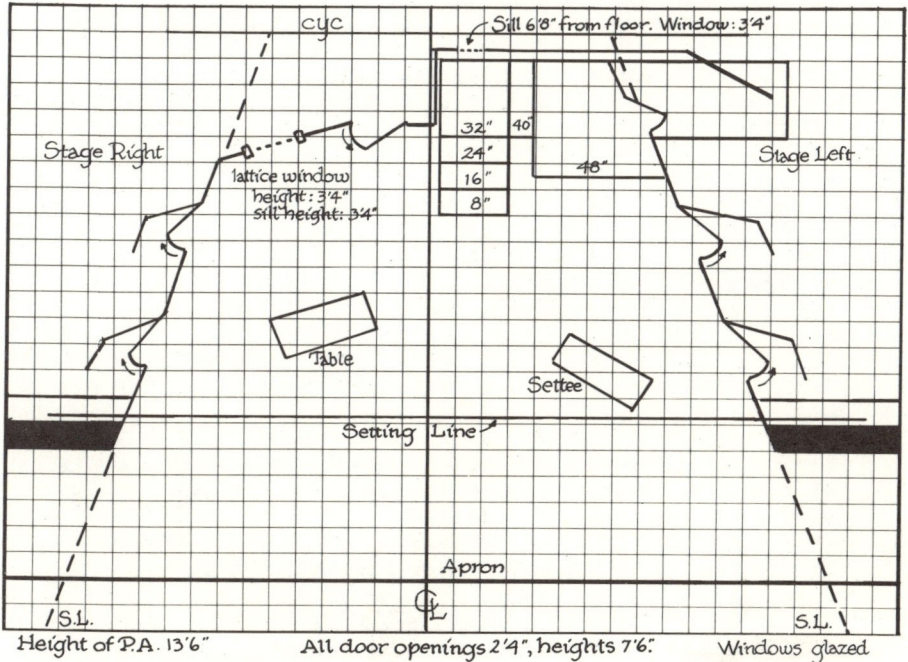

13. Ground plan for *Rookery Nook* design.   —S. MacGregor.

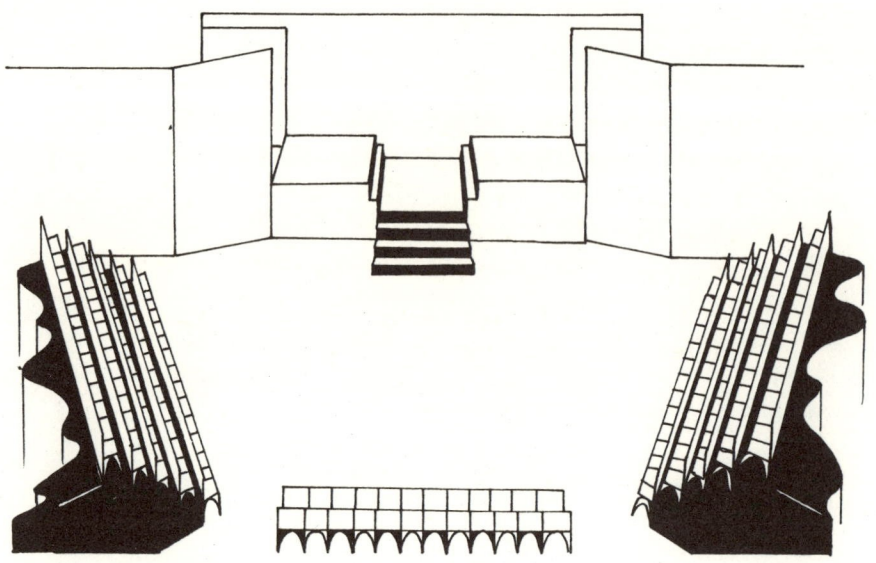

14. Set design for *The Yeomen of the Guard*.

15. Ground plan for *The Yeomen of the Guard* design. —S.MacGregor.

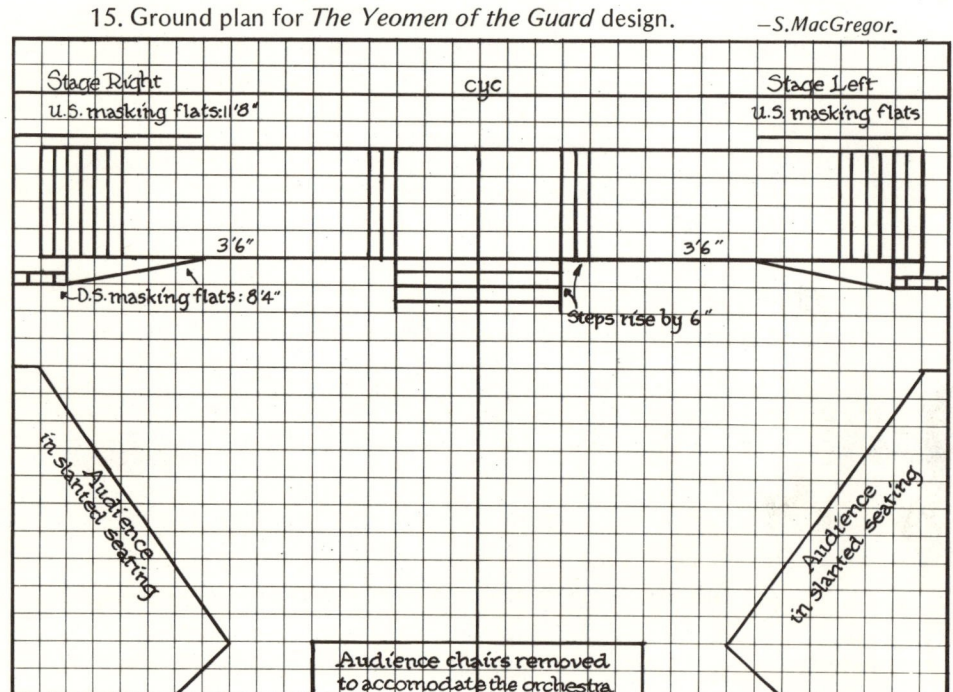

Scenery—Design and Building

allowing plenty of space for them to move about in. The ground plan shows the four large entrances to the back and sides. The white cyc was left open and was colorfully lit. Notice the black masking flats in illustration 12, called *returns,* which go from the downstage edge of the set into the wings, leaving access for the stage crew to alter props and furniture.

These ground plans (illustrations 13 and 15) are made in exactly the same way as the type shown in the last section, with the addition of lines to represent the position of the flats and the platforms. It is helpful if the lines are drawn in with a colored felt tip pen—one color for the flats and a different one for the platforms. The dimensions are the real, not scale, sizes of doors, heights of the platforms, sizes of windows and the height of their sills from the stage floor.

An important point to note is how the atmosphere of a play can be helped by the positioning of the set in relation to the sight and center lines. The set in illustration 12 is placed symmetrically on the stage—the center line cuts the set into two equal halves, and helps to create the rigid and solemn atmosphere. An effect of coziness and relaxation can be achieved by placing the set off center and allowing the walls to "bulge" away from the sight lines. This also makes a more interesting picture. The positioning of scenery and furniture should always be experimented with before the final design is agreed upon, and that is best done with a model, made to scale and built up on a basic ground plan of the stage. This gives freedom to experiment not only with the positioning of the scenery, but with the platforms, and later on, the furniture.

The "walls" of the set, containing doors and windows, are marked out on thin cardboard to the scale you are using, and then cut out and stood up with a support taped onto the back. Make the walls the correct height to scale. The thin cardboard can be bent quite easily, enabling you to experiment with the shape of the set. Cut out the doors and windows so that you can see where the masking flats are to be positioned. Take care to leave enough space for actors to get between the masking flats and the back of the actual set. When you are satisfied with your design, glue the bottom edge of the cardboard walls to the appropriate places on your ground plan. (Illustration 16.) Platforms can be made out of cardboard or cut out of pieces of styrofoam and glued to the ground plan.

Sets can be most effective if designed with a variety of platforms, using plainly painted flats to mask the wings on a proscenium stage. Raised platform blocks can be built up to create interesting shapes, and as long as your design reflects the atmosphere of the play, it is unneccessary to have complicated

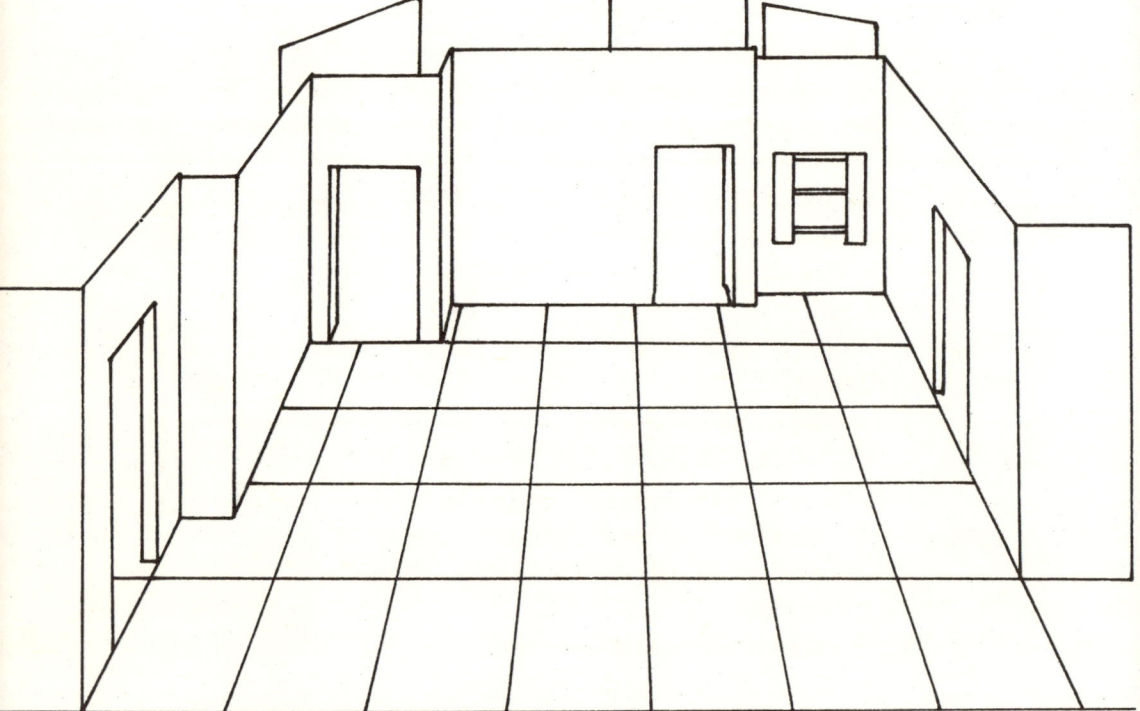

16. Cardboard set glued to ground plan.

Scenery—Design and Building

box sets, which take time and trouble to build, and which also are expensive.

Scenery design is most effective when it is simple, and simplicity should always be your first thought. The only rule to remember when using blocks or different platforms is that they should be at their highest upstage, except when used for in-the-round when the platforms should be at their highest towards the center, without obscuring any of the audience's view. If you are going to use blocks to break up an acting area and create more interest, experiment with their positioning, to scale, on a model first. It will save time and trouble.

SCENERY BUILDING

Scenery is traditionally made of wooden frames with canvas or a substitute material, such as muslin, stretched over it. The construction, called a *flat,* is easy to erect and keep in place, relatively lightweight and takes up little room when stored. Flats can be made to any height and width required, but do not really need to be more than four feet wide for ease in handling. To make a flat twelve feet high and three feet wide you will require the following materials:

For the framework:

- two 12-foot lengths of lumber approximately 3 inches wide by 1 inch, planed
- four 3-foot lengths of lumber approximately 3 inches wide by 1 inch, planed
- two pieces of ¼-inch plywood, each 6 inches square
- sixteen corrugated fasteners
- about a half pound of tacks, three-quarters of an inch long
- small quantity of wood glue

For the cover:
>large piece of canvas or muslin
>one pound of carpenter's glue
>tacks
>old paintbrush
>sharp trimming knife

After planing at the lumber yard, the width and thickness of the timber may be a little less than that required, but the difference is slight and is no cause for concern. The ends of the timber MUST be square, so it is wise to buy timbers slightly longer than you need and to cut them to size yourself, with a saw, making sure your cuts are as accurate as possible. Place the two 12-foot lengths on the floor parallel to each other with the two shorter 3-foot lengths at each end. (Illustration 17.) Use a

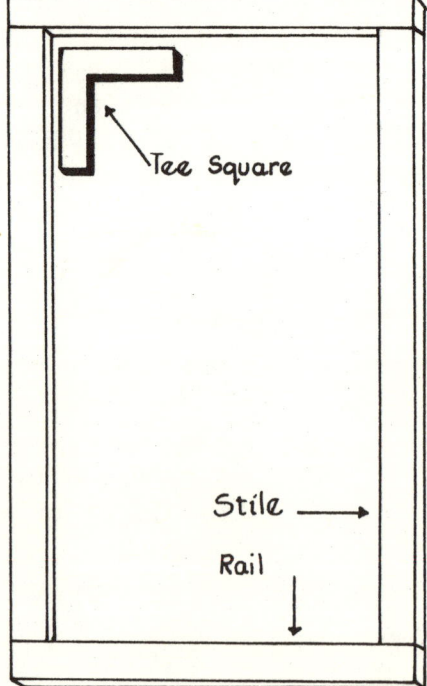

17. Timbers laid out ready for constructing the flat.

18. Joining timber with corrugated fasteners.

tee-square to ensure that the pieces butt tightly to each other at a right angle. Hammer two corrugated fasteners into each joint flush with the surface of the timber. (Illustration 18.) Cut the two remaining 3-foot pieces so that they fit snugly between the stiles at equal distances from the top and bottom rails. Make sure they are at right angles to the stiles and secure them with a couple of corrugated fasteners on each side. Now take the pieces of plywood and cut them diagonally. Smear a small amount of the carpenter's glue over one side of each of the plywood triangles and fix them to the four corners of the frame about one-quarter of an inch from the edges. Lastly, tack them to the frame. (Illustration 19.) Leave it for about twelve hours to dry.

The frame now needs to be covered. Begin by turning the frame over so that the plywood triangles are underneath. Do not fix the canvas to them because they will make wrinkles at each corner. Place the material on the frame making sure that you have a slight overhang at each edge. Make a small diagonal cut at each corner to ensure that the canvas lies on the frame without creasing. Tack the canvas to the frame by starting in the CENTER OF A STILE and move towards one end, then go

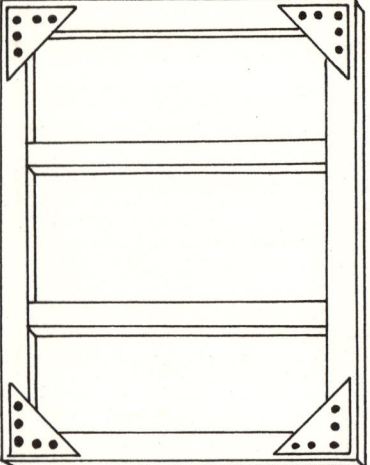

19. Tacking the plywood triangles to the corners of the flat to insure it remains rigid.

back to the center and work towards the other end, pulling the canvas lightly towards the direction you are moving. Do the same on the other stile, pulling the canvas not only in the direction you are moving but towards you as well. (Illustration 20.) Repeat the procedure for each rail at either end, but do not tack the canvas onto the central rails. The tacks should be

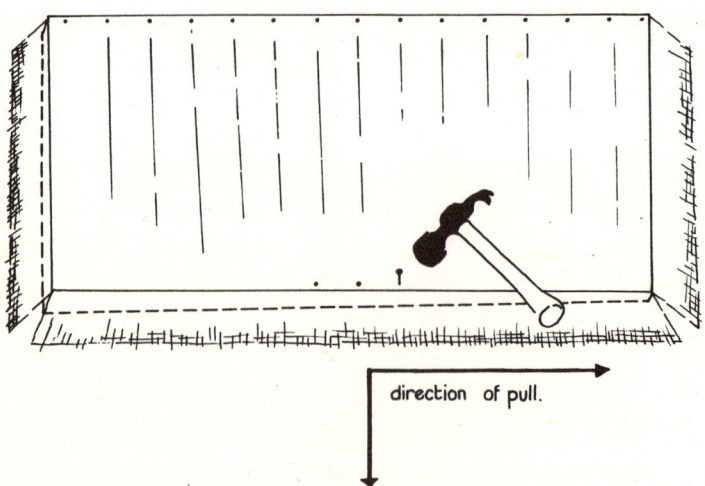

direction of pull.

20. Canvassing a flat. Keep the canvas fairly tight by pulling in the direction of the arrows while tacking it to the frame.

Scenery—Design and Building

hammered in at intervals of about four inches and about two inches in from the outside edge.

Apply carpenter's glue by lifting the edge of the canvas back, and painting it onto the exposed timber. Press the canvas down with a damp sponge and leave until the glue has set, normally about six hours, and then cut off the surplus canvas with a trimming knife, making the cut about three-quarters of an inch from the edge of the timber.

This is the simplest method of making a plain scenery flat. Canvas is the best material to use for covering but it is expensive. However, as it is sold already fireproofed, and as all scenery and curtains MUST be fireproofed before a performance, a lot of time and trouble can be saved by using it. Muslin is cheaper but does not last as long. It is not fireproofed when sold and would have to be treated with special chemicals obtainable from suppliers of scenery-making equipment and paint.

Before the flats are erected as part of the scenery on the stage, they need to be *sized*. This is a type of glue which helps the paint to stay on the flat, and fills the pores of the material. It is made by mixing one pound of size into a gallon of water and heating. It must be stirred constantly to prevent the size from burning, and when thoroughly mixed should be applied to the material of the flat with a paint brush. Because muslin has such large pores in the weave, powdered whiting should be added to the size when it is being mixed. This will prime the flat and help fill the pores. When dry, the material will be very taut.

Variations on the plain flat are shown on pages 36 and 37. It is not difficult to see the slight alterations made in construction. Illustration 21 is a window flat. The lattice work is made by fixing thin pieces of wood or tape with drawing pins to the frame. Take care to space the lattice work equally. Should you require "glass" the window space may either be left open, or

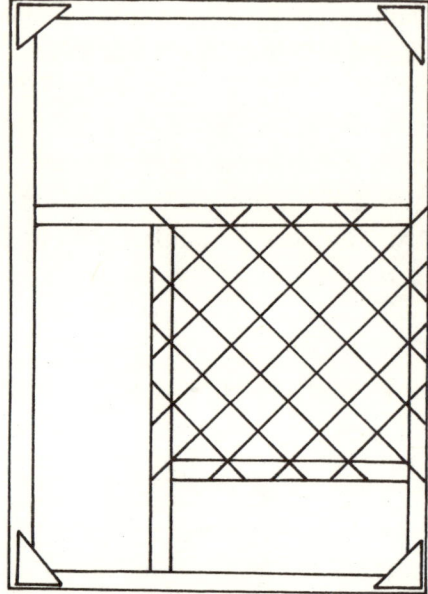

21. A window flat.

glazed with a sheet of transparent frost which is one of the many types of color medium used to filter stage lighting. Illustration 22 is a door flat. The door, which is a separate, smaller flat hinged to the main structure must be covered and painted on BOTH sides. The door "sill" is a thin strip of metal screwed into the bottom ends of the stiles. Fix the door to the flat by laying the flat facedown on the stage, and insert the door into the open space. Hinges can then be positioned and fixed by screws onto the door and the flat. In the diagram the door opens away from the wings onto the stage and when closed is prevented from swinging into the wings by the doorstop fixed to the flat. Should the door need to open into the wings then the stop must be fixed to the onstage edge of the door (out of sight in the diagram). A ball-and-socket catch should be used to fasten the door, and a door handle fixed to each side.

A fireplace flat (illustration 23) is made by constructing a

Scenery—Design and Building

22. A door flat. Notice the thin piece of wood fixed to the edge of the flat to prevent the door from being pushed.

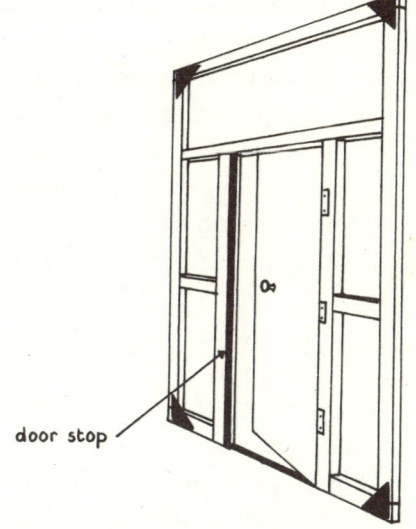

flat with an opening at the bottom end and fixing a shallow plywood "box" over the opening. A piece of wood four inches wide is screwed onto the rail above the opening to form a

23. A fireplace flat.

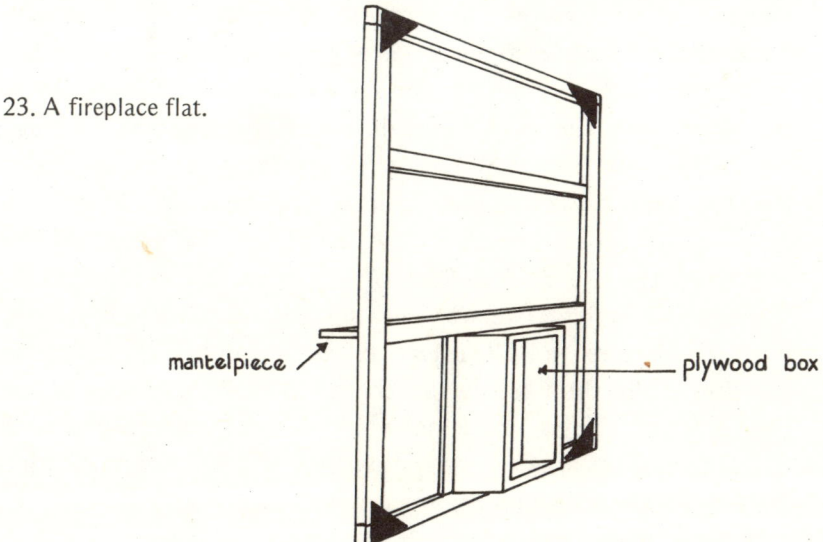

mantelpiece. Drive the screws into the mantelpiece from the back of the flat.

All sorts of decorative cut-outs and shapes may be fixed to flats to give them a greater sense of depth, but do not use any material which cannot be fireproofed easily. Contact your local fire department headquarters if ever you are in doubt about fireproofing and fire regulations.

With experiment and planning a plain flat or a masking flat can be given a lot of depth and a great deal of reality merely by painting with scenic powder paint. The design should be sketched out with charcoal or chalk when the entire set has been assembled. Always use a straight edge for painting lines, and remember that the design needs to be about three times larger than it would be in real life.

Mix powder paint into a paste with cold water, according to the supplier's directions, and work into a thin cream by adding liquid size. The size will prevent the paint from flaking when it is dry. Old flats may be reused merely by priming them again but they must be prepared first by scrubbing off any flaky paint and gluing patches over any holes. NEVER paint a flat with domestic paint; emulsion is too heavy and an oil based paint is a fire hazard. Before painting, the set should be erected firmly on the stage, and this is done with a couple of extending *stage braces* and *weights,* as shown in illustration 24. The hooks at the top end of the brace fit into eyelets which have been screwed into the stiles about two-thirds of the height of the flat from the floor. The foot of the brace is firmly held by slotting the weight over it. The flat should tilt slightly away from the braces and NOT lean on them, and when correctly positioned the thumbscrews in the middle of the braces should be tightened. If you have no weights, small sacks filled with dry sand are just as good, providing they are heavy enough. Illustration 25 shows a *French brace* which is an alternative to the extending brace and is simple to make. All flats and blocks

Scenery—Design and Building

24. Erecting a flat with stage weights and braces.
    —*David Richardson, reproduced by permission of Mr. J.K. Wilkinson.*

should be secured to the stage with weights—not screws or nails. A *book flat* can be made by hinging the edges of two flats together. It is virtually self-supporting, and is a sturdy and effective method of fixing the downstage flats to the returns. The gap between the edges should be covered with a narrow strip of canvas glued to the "onstage" side. The whole set is made more firm and gaps between the edges of the flats eliminated, by a process called *cleating* (illustration 26).

Other pieces of scenery like pillars and trees can be made by cutting out plywood shapes and fixing them to a framework, but unless the effect is intentional they look false and uninteresting. A round shape like the pillar in illustration 27 is made with four semicircular pieces of timber about three-quarters of an inch thick, to which four lengths of timber (the height of the pillar), each one inch by two inches, are glued and screwed round the circular edge. Canvas is glued and tacked over the framework

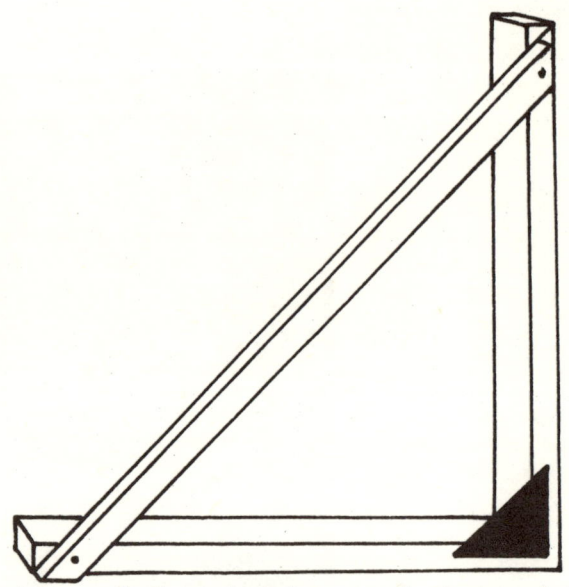

25. A French brace. Easily made and very sturdy, the brace is fixed to the flat with hinges so that it can be folded back for easy storage. Like the extending brace, it should be two-thirds of the height of the flat it is supporting.

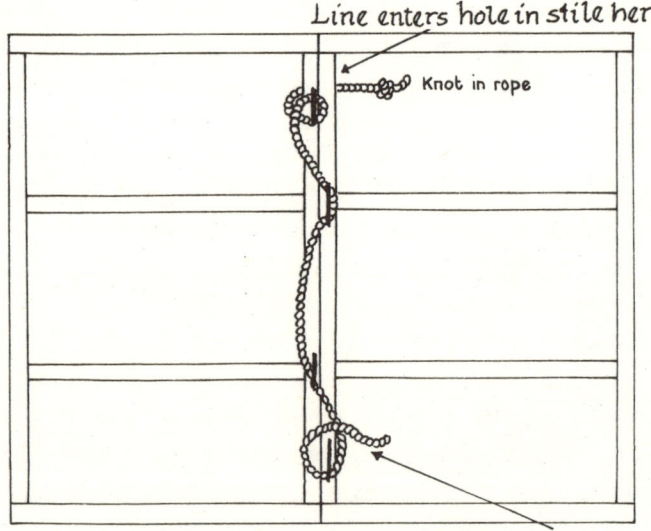

26. Cleating a flat with rope.

and then sized. A plywood decoration is put on the top and a small base at the bottom. Careful painting completes the illusion of a real pillar.

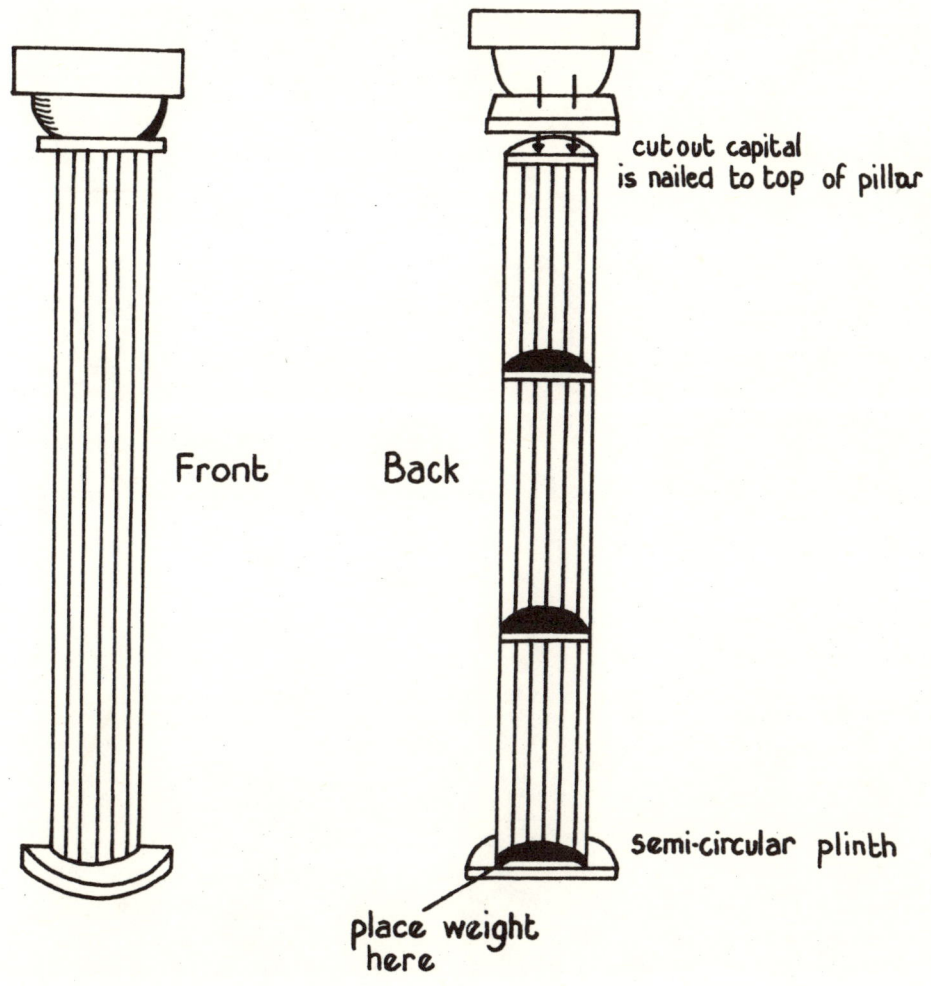

27. Construction of a pillar.

Because of the need for expensive materials, a workshop, and tools, you will probably only get a chance to do this work if you are lucky enough to be in a team helping to build the set for a production. But there is nothing to stop you from choosing a play and designing a set for it, using a model and a ground plan. If you have access to blocks, you can design a set using platforms only and actually building up a real design.

FURNITURE AND PROPS

Furniture, like scenery, should always fit the style and historical period of a play. Very often it is possible to pick up chairs, tables, and even sofas quite inexpensively in junk shops or at yard sales, and sometimes people are only too pleased to get rid of such items that are worn or damaged, without charging for them. Furniture which is of some value or good quality should not be used on the stage, because it easily becomes damaged. You will not have to worry about a worthless piece of junk, which can be repaired or altered to resemble the style of furniture you require, and if cleaned down with sandpaper or steel wool, can be painted with scenic powder paint mixed with size.

If you are dealing with a period play, you will have to look for pictures of the type of furniture popular at the time the play is set. The local library is the best source of information for this. Tables that look heavy and solid are difficult to find, but a modern kitchen table can be transformed to look old and substantial, by completely covering it with a dark-colored plain cloth or drape. Old sofas can be "recovered" by cutting out cloth to fit the shape roughly and pinning it into place.

Your ground plan must naturally include the positions of any

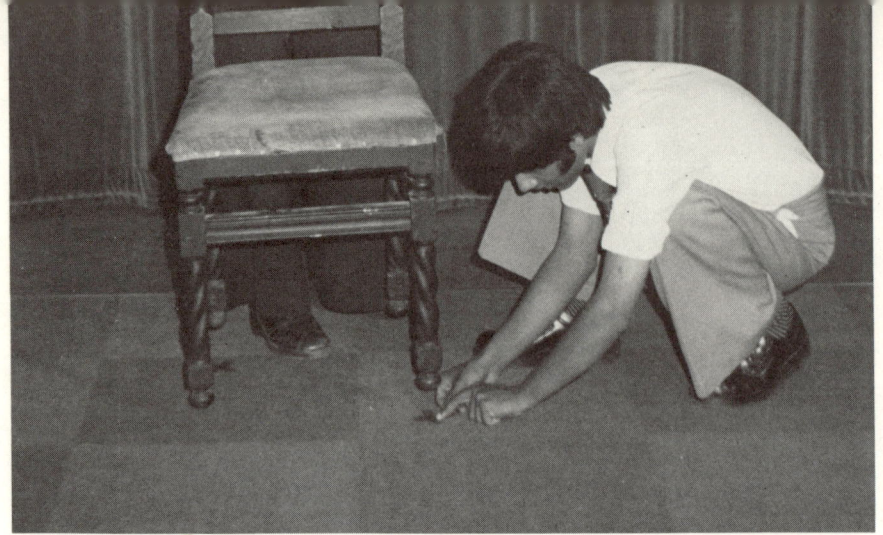

28. Taping the position of a chair. It is only necessary to tape the position of two of the legs, as long as you know to which legs the marks refer. This method can be used for all pieces of furniture.
—*David Richardson, reproduced by permission of Mr. J. K. Wilkinson.*

furniture, and this is done by marking the shapes of the various pieces on the plan. If you look back at illustration 13, you can see how the table and couch have been drawn in.

Actors become frustrated and bewildered if the stage furniture is placed in a slightly different position for each rehearsal, so it is necessary to mark on the stage exactly where each piece is to be positioned. This is best done with colored tape. It is easy to see and will not harm the surface of the stage. Illustration 28 shows how this method can be used for all pieces of furniture. For plays which are divided into several acts, and which require furniture to be repositioned, it helps to use a different colored tape for each act. For example, furniture positions for act 1 might be in black, act 2 in red, and act 3 in blue. This will enable the stage crew to reset the furniture quickly and without fuss. But great care must be taken not to get the colors mixed!

When designing a set you should try and have a complete picture of it in your mind. If, for example, it is of the interior of a room, thought should be given to the inclusion of articles such as hat stands, cushions, pictures, mirrors, light switches, and ashtrays. It is sometimes difficult to decide whether these articles are scenery or furniture. However, if they are important enough to be for special use by the actors during the play, such articles are called *props*.

Furniture and Props 45

29. This is a simple set design built up on a proscenium arch stage. It has several characteristics already discussed. Platforms are created by using blocks of different heights. The pillars were purposefully made to look flat and unreal, yet are effective because they contrast with the white cyc behind them. The table and chairs were originally "junk," patched up and painted. Note the way they are angled on the stage. The stage, however, is badly "dressed." For example, two spotlights are showing which is a distraction when all the others are carefully hidden, and the border tabs do not hang perfectly straight—details which need attending to if you want to achieve a first-rate presentation.

—*David Richardson, reproduced by permission of Mr. J. K. Wilkinson.*

PROPS

This is an abbreviation of "hand properties," small articles to be used and handled by the actors during a play. There are two types of props, *personal props,* which are taken onto the stage by the actor, and *stage props,* which are set on the stage, ready for use, before the play begins. To prevent loss or damage, it is advisable to have a *props master* and an assistant who are responsible for the overall care of all props.

Personal props should be laid out on a table backstage, ready to hand to the actor before he enters the stage. Any props brought off the stage should always be returned to the props table—small objects can easily be lost by a nervous actor who might absentmindedly take them with him to the dressing room! A proscenium stage should have a props table in both the stage left and stage right wings, if there are to be entrances from both sides of the stage. The tables should always be tidy and well-organized, because disaster can strike if a prop for the opening of a play happens to be buried under a pile of objects which are not needed until much later on. It is also the duty of the props master to set the stage props accurately before either a rehearsal or a performance begins, so it would be helpful to make a *props plot* like the one shown in illustration 30. As you can see, it is a rough ground plan of the set, and does not need to be drawn to scale. The positioning of the props needs to be marked on it as accurately as possible.

The props themselves should be real, but sometimes, as in the case of knives or guns, this is not possible or desirable. Instead a substitute must be found that looks like the real thing, and if it cannot be found it must be made. You can have a lot of fun making the props for a play, preferably out of materials that are strong and lightweight and which can be painted effectively to look convincing. Papier mâché, which is made by soaking strips of newspaper in wallpaper adhesive and laying the

Furniture and Props

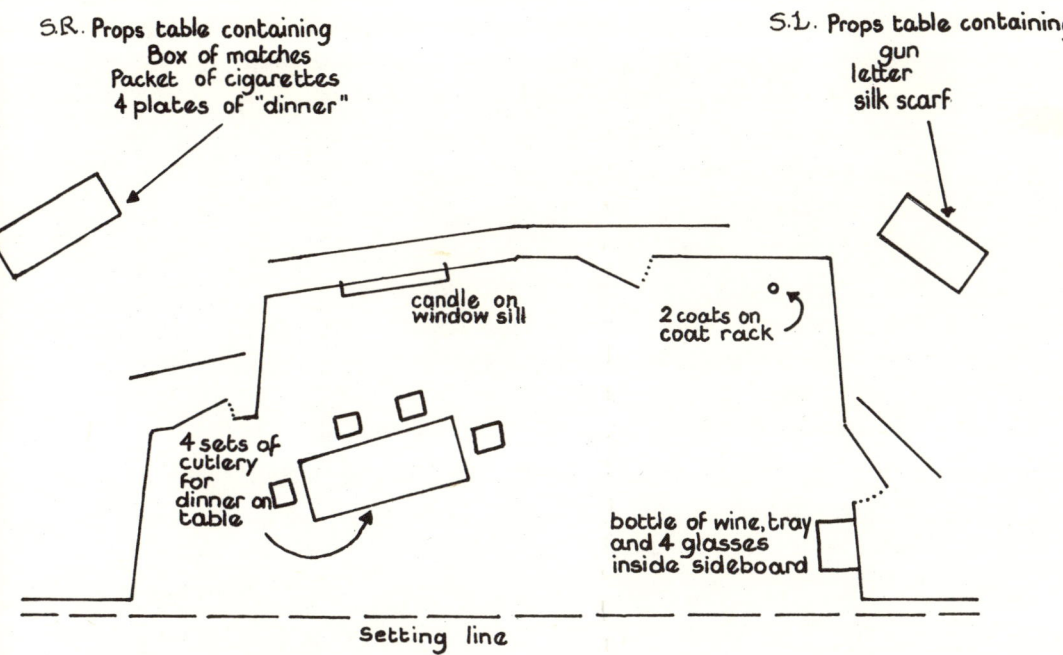

30. A props plot.

strips over a basic framework until you have built up a shape, is, when thoroughly dry, a strong and lightweight material. If it is coated liberally with a plastic liquid, it will have a smooth glossy finish when painted. Of course there are other materials which can be used to make convincing props, and you will find it fun to experiment for yourself. Lumps of rock or stone can be made out of thick pieces of dark grey foam rubber, which are easy to store, too. Old documents or parchment are made by soaking paper in vinegar and baking in a moderate oven for about ten minutes. Helmets can be made by covering a balloon with papier mâché. When you have made the shape that you need, and the material is thoroughly dry, the balloon is removed by bursting it. The helmet will then need to be painted. Precious stones and jewelry can be made from papier mâché. They should be made separately, and are very effective if treated with a plastic liquid when dry. They can then be painted in bright blue, red, or green. Swords and daggers can be made from pieces of wood, carefully shaped and painted. Aerosol paint sprays give the best finish and are easy to use. When painting a sword blade, spray it with silver paint first, and when it is dry spray it lightly again with black. This will give the blade a metallic appearance. Decorate the handle by twisting a piece of thick rope around it, which should be held in place with a spot of glue. Paint the rope with some gold lacquer.

If you need to make a shield, start with a circular piece of thick cardboard about three feet in diameter, and cut a slit from the center to the edge. Overlap the two ends to form a concave shape and tape firmly. Now build up a thick layer of papier mâché on the outside of the cardboard, by covering it with long strips as shown in illustration 31. Curl the papier mâché round the edges of the cardboard to form a rim. You can build up the shield as much or as little as you require. Before

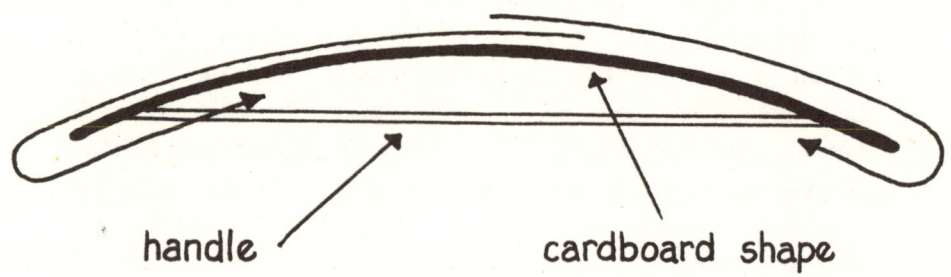

31. Making a shield.

Furniture and Props

the papier mâché is dry, sew a couple of thick tapes to the inside of the shield. You will need strong yarn and a needle to pull the yarn through. When the shield is thoroughly dry, the tapes, which are for holding the shield, will be kept firmly in place. You can then decorate the shield by gluing on shapes made out of any spare material, such as cardboard, rope, or styrofoam. Finish by painting the shield on BOTH sides.

If a meal has to be provided on stage, it is best to give the actors something real that they can eat. Sliced or chopped fruit such as an apple or banana will do, but place it on the plate as if it were a meal. Never make a stage meal up from anything that crumbles, such as biscuit or cake, because this could choke the unfortunate actor.

Many plays require lanterns or candles, but it is dangerous to use naked flames on the stage. The lantern and candle described here both work off flashlight batteries, and are quite safe. You may like to make these props. They will take a little time, but if you make them carefully and look after them, they will last as long as you want them to. To make the lantern you will

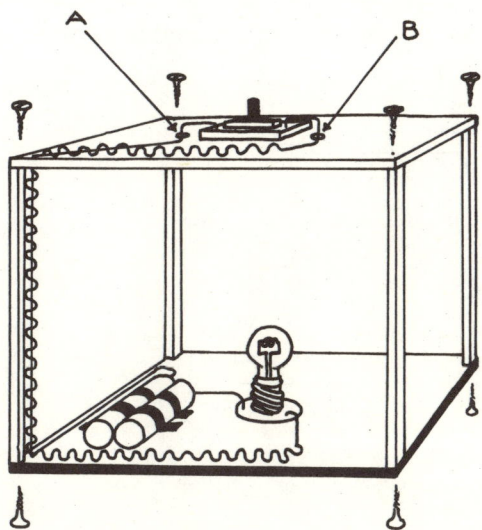

32. Construction of a prop lantern.

need a flashlight bulb rated at 3.5 volts, a 4½-volt battery, a bulb holder, a small press switch, and about eighteen inches of 2-conductor bell wire. Illustration 32 shows how the lantern is put together. The top and base are made of two pieces of timber about five inches by five inches and one-half of an inch thick. The supports are made from four pieces of timber, each six inches long and three-quarters of an inch thick. Fix the top and base to the supports with wood glue and long thin screws. Drill a hole slightly less than the diameter of the screw beforehand, to prevent the wood from splitting. The switch should be mounted right in the center and held in place with a dab of all-purpose glue. Drill holes at "A" and "B" for the wire to pass through the top. The wire should be pulled tightly, taped to the underside of the top, passed down, and taped to one of the supports. Illustration 33 shows you how to connect the wires. The battery is held in place by elastic bands, pinned to the base with drawing pins. The bulb holder can be screwed down. Illustration 34 shows how to complete the top. A piece of wood is used the same size as the top, but with a thickness equal to the height of the switch. It needs to have a piece cut out of the center to fit snugly around the switch, and is secured

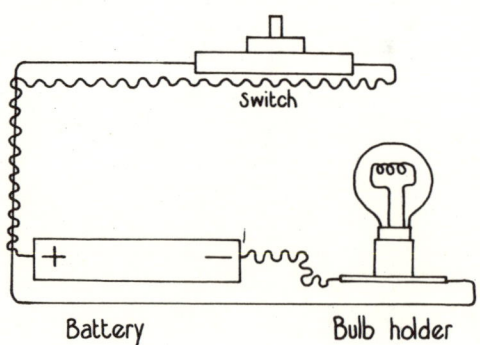

33. Wiring diagram for lantern.

Furniture and Props

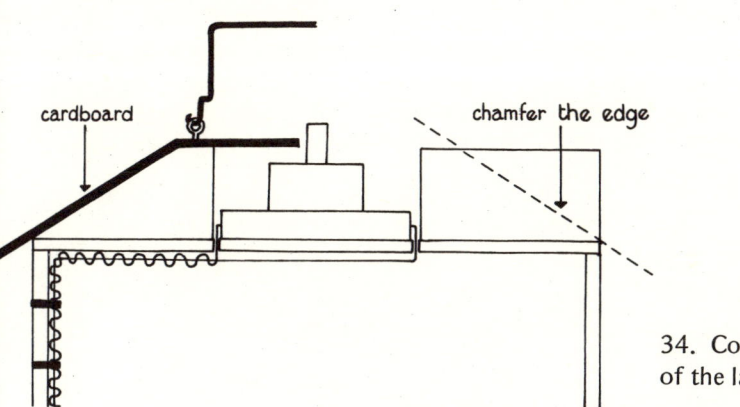

34. Completing the top of the lantern.

to the top with glue and screws. Once the edges have been beveled, pieces of card can be stuck on to form the "roof." Small eyelets are screwed in as shown and a handle made out of a piece of thick wire, bent to shape. The lantern is finished off by wrapping tracing paper all around and gluing it to each support. Black insulation tape can be used to give a window effect. The bottom "rail" needs to be wide enough to hide the battery. Paint the cardboard "roof" and the button on the switch black, and the lantern is finished.

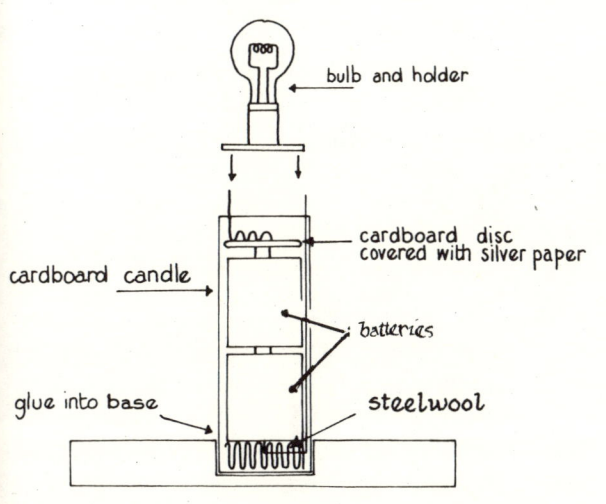

35. Construction of a prop candle.

The candle requires the same electrical fittings with the exception of the press switch. You will also need two flashlight batteries (illustration 35). Make a cylinder out of cardboard that is the combined height of the two batteries and the bulb holder. Tape the edges securely. The cylinder will have to be the same diameter as the base of the bulb holder. Take a piece of circular board which is about one-and-a-quarter inch thick and bore a hole the diameter of the "candle" about three quarters of the way through. Glue the "candle" into the base. Attach one end of a piece of wire to a small quantity of steel wool and insert this into the base, letting the other end of the wire stick out of the top. Insert the two batteries as shown, and over them place a disc of cardboard covered with silver paper. A piece of wire should be securely fixed to the cardboard and the silver paper. Place the bulb holder on the disc so that only the bulb is visible and connect each piece of wire to the connections on the bulb holder. Secure the bulb holder to the top of the "candle" with strong adhesive tape. The candle is made to go "on" by screwing the bulb in tightly, and "off" by unscrewing it about half a turn. A handle can be made out of a piece of shaped wood screwed to the base. When the candle and the base are painted, the prop is finished.

When making the electrical connections for these two props, always remove a small amount (about one-half of an inch) of the insulation, so that the bare wires connect with the electrical components.

STAGE LIGHTING

There are two main reasons for using specialized lighting on the stage. The first is to ensure that the actor can be seen clearly and the second is to enable the appropriate atmosphere of a play to be established. To achieve this we use instruments which have inside them powerful *lamps* (NOT bulbs) to produce a highly intense light. Illustrations 36, 37, and 38 illustrate the type of instruments generally found on most stages. Illustration 36 shows an *ellipsoidal spot*, which is constructed to project a hard-edged beam of light. The shape of the beam is made by inserting one of the metal diaphragms, that are supplied with this type of lantern, into the slot where the "barrel" sticks out of the lamp casing. Different makes of profile spots have slightly different methods for narrowing the aperture through which light passes, but the principle is the same. At the front of the "barrel" is a lens which can be moved in or out to focus the light into a well-defined beam. When focused correctly the screw on the side of the case should be tightened to prevent the lens from slipping out of adjustment.

Illustration 37 shows a *fresnel spot*, which gives a soft-edged pool of light. Adjustment is made by loosening the screw on the

36. An ellipsoidal spot. —*Photograph courtesy of Berkey Colortran, Division of Berkey Photo.*

underside of the case and pushing it forward to give a wide beam, or pulling it back to give a narrow beam.

Illustration 38 shows a *scoop*, which, as its name suggests, floods light generally over the area on which it is directed. It cannot spot a particular area of the stage. Illustration 39 is of a *batten*, which is like a series of floods placed side by side. It is wired up into three independent circuits, so that every third compartment all the way along

37. A fresnel spot. —*Photograph courtesy of Berkey Colortran, Division of Berkey Photo.*

38. A scoop. —*Photograph courtesy of Berkey Colortran, Division of Berkey Photo.*

lights up independently of the other two circuits. The batten is often found on proscenium stages, and is especially useful for general lighting, or for lighting the cyc with three colors.

Whatever type of stage is being lit, the instruments should be positioned well above the performers' heads and secured with a hook clamp, either to brackets which are fixed to the walls or to lengths of steel tubing especially provided for the instruments to hang from. If there are none of these facilities, the instruments must be placed securely on telescopic stands, so that they shine down, at an angle, onto the acting area. Instruments should never be allowed to shine vertically straight down because this makes the lamps burn out quickly, and they are expensive items to replace. For a proscenium stage the instruments should be erected so that they shine from the front AND the side. This arrangement will help to produce a three-dimensional effect and completely illuminate the face of the actor. For an arena stage the instruments can be positioned to light from the three sides. An in-the-round stage would need to have lights positioned from all four sides.

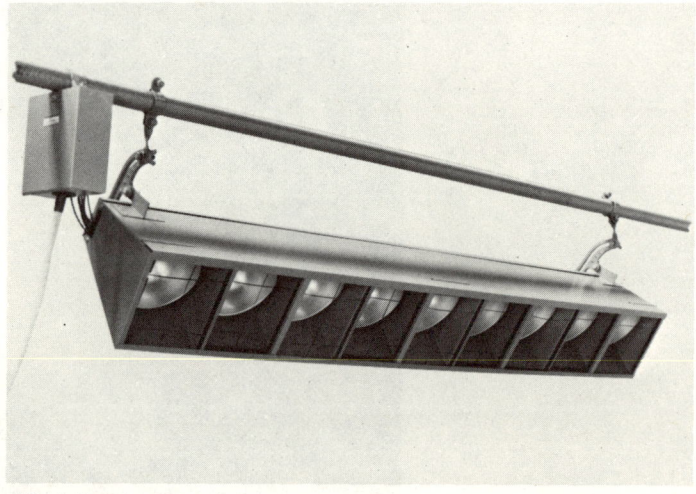

39. A batten. —W.J. Furse & Co., Ltd.

Stage Lighting 57

An instrument is adjusted (or angled) by loosening the nut which holds it to the C-clamp. This will enable it to be swivelled around, while the tilt is controlled by loosening the thumb screw at the side of the casing. The nut and the thumb screw should be tightened when the correct angle has been made.

COLOR MEDIUM

This is made out of a transparent plastic material. Its purpose is to filter the ordinary white light into color. It is obtainable from stage-lighting firms (some of which are listed at the end of this book) in sheets of various sizes. For a small charge you can buy a sample booklet from a lighting company, and see for yourself the many colors and shades that are manufactured. The choice of color is naturally a very important one, and it is often necessary to experiment before you hit on the right color for the atmosphere you are trying to create. Never use a color unless it "feels" right—because if you are not happy with it, the chances are that the audience will not be either.

The color medium can be cut with scissors, and should slide easily into the color frame without buckling and fit to size leaving no gaps around the edges.

LIGHTING A PLAY

You should always begin by knowing the play you are going to light. If possible, read it through and watch the early rehearsals because then you can judge exactly where the main acting areas are. They are the parts of the stage where the most important events occur. Whenever possible light each acting area, and especially the faces of the actors in it, with TWO spots as shown in illustration 40. It is impossible to light everybody all of the time. A crowd, for example, may have to be lit

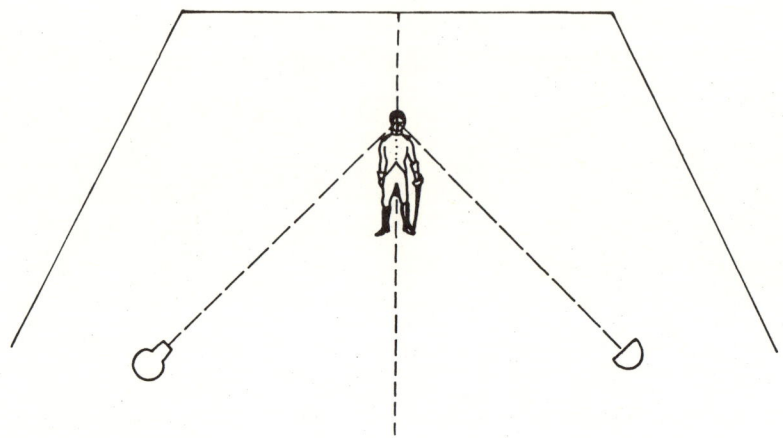

40. Lighting an actor. The two lights should each be angled at 45° to the face of the actor.

with only one spot. Often there is a small amount of overspill from each spot sufficient to illuminate other characters and parts of the set. But the angling of your lights must take into account the atmosphere you want to create. Not every set needs to be bathed in light, and sometimes you may have to create pools of light and areas of shadow. Once you have decided where the main acting areas are and feel you know the type of atmosphere the lighting must give, it is necessary to make a *lighting plot,* but it cannot be made until the set has been designed. Neither can the lights be fixed up and angled onto the actors faces in the main acting areas until the set is built and in position, and you cannot make a final decision about the colors you may want to use until the set is painted, because the wrong choice of color medium could drastically alter the color of the set.

The lighting plot is, to begin with, a plan of what you think the lighting should be like. Naturally, as a play reaches its final rehearsals your plot will become altered as your ideas change, and once the play is performed the plot becomes a record of what you have done. All the information about the lighting is

Stage Lighting

therefore put on the plot, including any changes of color that may have to be made during the course of the play, but for the sake of simplicity, color changes should be kept to the minimum, and should never be made to lights suspended above the audience.

Illustration 41 is a lighting plot based on the set design shown for *Rookery Nook* on page 26. The circles represent pools of light from the spots. The three-sided shapes backstage represent floodlights placed on stands, which would be needed to provide the effect of daylight seen through the windows, or the light from a room when one of the doors was opened. As the set is the inside of a room, more general light is needed. A note of this is written on the plot together with the colors used. Further information can be written inside the circles: an arrow to indicate from which direction the light is shining, the name and number of the color medium and the "name" of the instrument.

The naming of instruments is an important part of lighting organization. Illustration 42 shows you how to go about it. Each of the suspension barrels above the stage and the instruments attached to them should be numbered. The instrument arrowed in the diagram, therefore, would be known as spot bar 2 number 3 (sp. b.2, no.3). Although illustration 42 is for a proscenium arch stage, the same method of organization should be used for any lighting rig that is set up over an acting area. Once the instruments have been suspended, they will have to be connected to a control board by long lengths of cable ending in a plug. Each plug from each cable should be labeled with the name of the instrument to which it is connected.

Now the lighting design on the plot needs to be transferred to the lights on the stage. The instruments need to be hung on the suspension bar connected to cable which must be "run" to wherever the control panel is situated, and then angled. For this three people will be required to help—one to switch the light on and off at the control panel, another to go up a

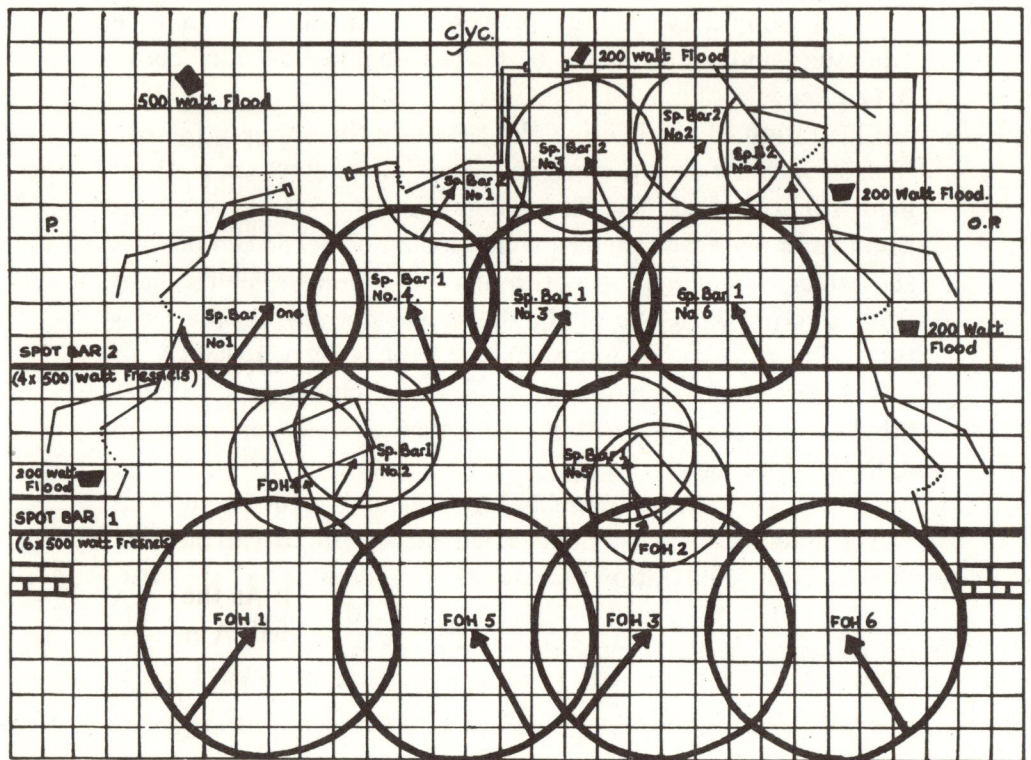

Colors: All spots with no. 36 (pale lavender) except for FOHs which have no. 3 (straw). Off-stage floods are open white (no color). In act 2 & 3 the floods shining on the cyc should have a no. 45 (daylight) inserted.

41. A lighting plot. This is complicated because it has so many spotlights. The set would still be reasonably well lit with half the number of lights, and all the spots on spot bar 1 could be replaced by a nine compartment batten (see illustration 39) colored alternately with no. 36 (pale lavender) and no. 3 (straw). Similarly the offstage floods are not absolutely essential, except for the two which shine on the cyc. The floods would be connected by cable and plugged into "dips" which are socket outlets fitted in the floor of most stages. The numbering and shades of the color medium are based on "Cinemoid" (see illustration 47).

Stage Lighting

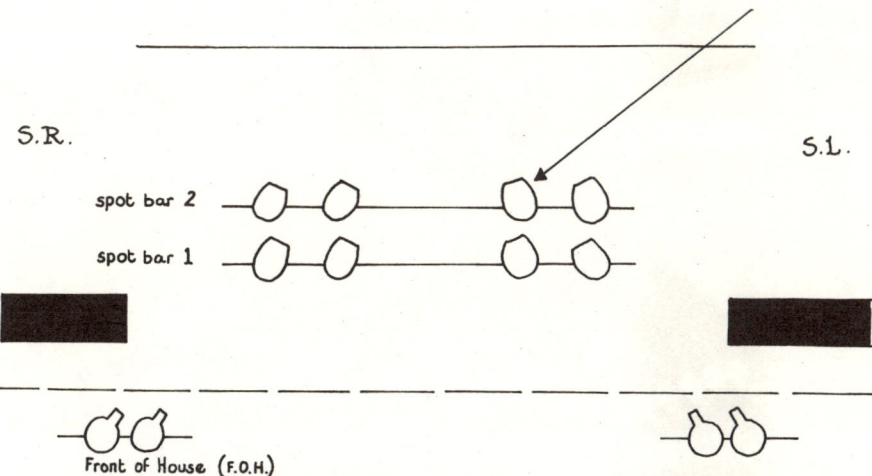

42. Naming of instruments. The instruments are numbered starting from stage right.

ladder to fix the lights, and a third to "stand in" as an actor and be lit at exactly the place you want the light to be angled. Each light must be angled separately and switched on just before it is angled, otherwise it will heat up and become impossible to touch. All other lights should be switched off. When the actors next assemble for a rehearsal, you can try out the lights to see if everything is working as you had planned. Probably some minor adjustments will have to be made, and any alterations should be shown on the lighting plot.

There are many different types of lighting control—illustrations 43 and 44 are two examples. Once the cable from an instrument has been plugged into a socket controlled by one of the sliding levers, that instrument will respond whenever the lever is moved. For both of the types shown, when the levers are right down, no electricity will be allowed to flow to the lamp so it will not shine, but as the lever is pushed up electricity will flow to the lamp and it will become bright. Because the levers control the brightness of the lamps and can make them fade up to their brightest or down until they are out, at any speed the operator

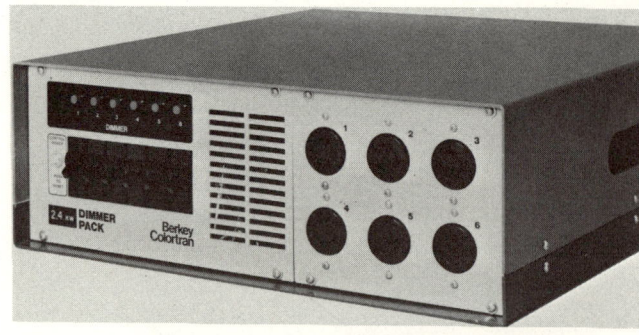

43. A lighting control unit.
—*Photograph courtesy of Berkey Colortran, Division of Berkey Photo.*

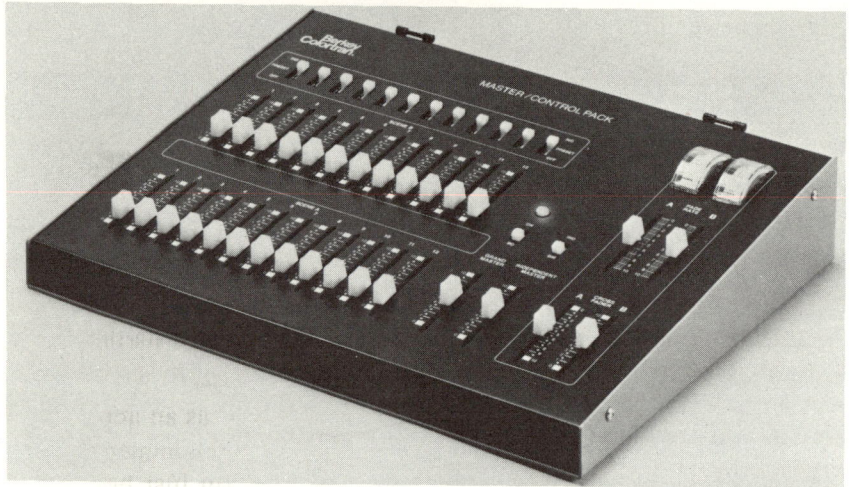

44. Remote control desk of a thyristor lighting unit. Thyristor controls are noiseless and easier to operate.
—*W. J. Furse & Co Ltd.*

wishes, the control board is sometimes called a *dimmer*. Most makes of dimmers do have switches too, so it is possible to switch off the instruments as well as dimming to off if you need to. Switching or dimming *all* instruments to off at the same time produces a *blackout*. For an experiment you should try fading in all the lights on stage very slowly and smoothly—say over three minutes—and then try a quick blackout. Similarly, if you angle four spots as shown in illustration 45, you can create a *cross fade,* which is shifting the light slowly from one acting area to another. This technique is especially useful in arena or in-the-round work. Illustration 46 illustrates a different type of cross fade.

Stage Lighting 63

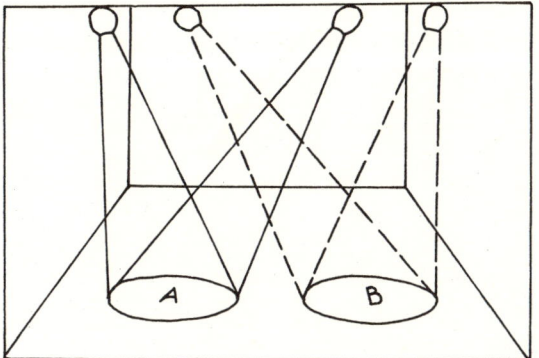

45. A cross fade. Slowly dim area "A" out while at the same time fading area "B" in.

46. A color cross fade. Only one area is lit, but it is lit with two contrasting colors. The dotted lines represent one color, the single lines another. An exciting effect can be obtained by changing the colors slowly on the same acting area.

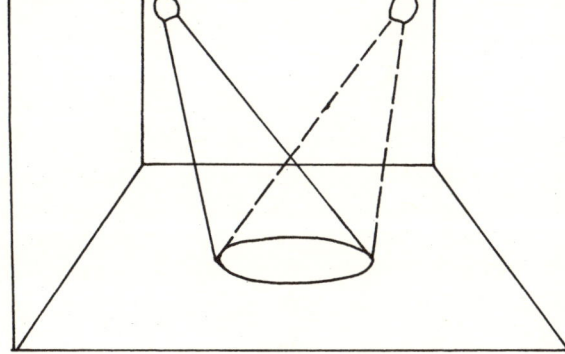

If you can use a proscenium stage with a cyclorama, a whole range of color cross fades can be created by projecting a batten or a series of floods to shine on the cyc. They should be set up as shown in illustration 47. The colors used should be primary colors so that when they are all on together at their brightest the effect of daylight is created. By careful fading up and dimming out it is possible to produce the effect of a cold light before dawn which grows into sunrise, blue sky or bright daylight, the approach of evening, dusk, and finally night. The effect on the cyc can be highlighted by altering the brightness of the instruments on stage, and a moon can be made by putting a small diaphragm in a profile spot and projecting it onto the cyc.

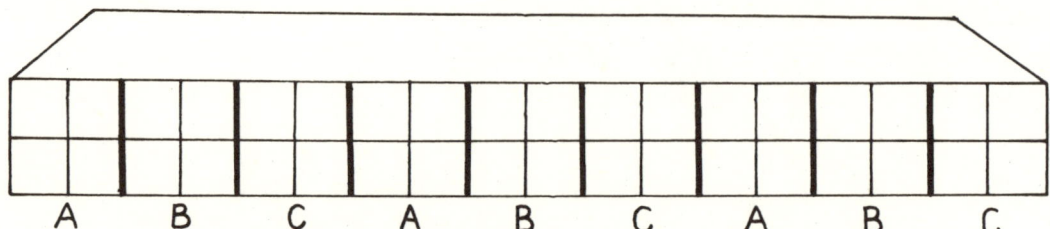

47. Setting up a batten with primary colors to give color effects on a cyclorama: A—primary red (6); B—primary green (39); C—primary blue (32). The numbering applies to "Cinemoid" color medium supplied by Strand Century. Note that these are subtractive primaries—not additive (pigment) primaries. School children are taught that the primaries are red, blue, and yellow.

When lighting a play, the lighting plot and subsequent angling is only the first stage of the job. We must remember that the lights will have to be controlled with great accuracy and a feeling for the play's atmosphere: The play must be run through from the beginning, and EVERY change made to the lighting

Cue	FoH				Spot Bar 1				Spot Bar 2				Cyc.			Remarks
	1	2	3	4	1	2	3	4	1	2	3	4	1Red	2Green	3Blue	
1		½		½		F			½	½				¼	¼	Up over 10 secs.
2	F	To Out	F	To Out	F	To Out	F	F	To Out	F	To Out	F	¾	½	½	Change over 20 mins.
3	Off		Off		Off		Off	Off	Off		Off		Off	Off	Off	Switched Blackout

48. A lighting cue sheet. If a cue signaling system (see page 69) is not being used, an extra column next to the cue number will have to be made to contain the actual words in the play when the lighting cues are to be given.

Stage Lighting 65

must be recorded. This is done by making out a cue sheet similar to illustration 48.

The cue sheet shows which dimmer operates which light, whether the light is to be put to on or off, and the amount of brightness required. The cue sheet also shows the speed at which lights must be altered, which is written in the remarks column. This column should also contain any other information that the *electrics operator* will need to know. In the example shown, cue 2 is a long fade up to give the effect of sunrise. If necessary, a line from the play may be written next to the cue number, and it is on this line, when it is spoken, that the cue must begin. All this is worked out at a *technical rehearsal* which is when specific alterations to the angling of the lamps have to be made. At the technical rehearsal a place would have to be found for such a cue to begin. It would be a little disconcerting (and probably funny for the audience) if the sun was seen to rise in about 30 seconds. If care is taken over a cue like this, the light will be seen to be increasing gradually on the stage over a long period of time, and when a remark is made by a character on the stage about dawn approaching, the line he has spoken will make sense and have purpose.

FINAL HINTS

Because light is a visual effect, it can be used to begin or end a play or scene without the need to open or shut curtains. It has the same effect of course, but somehow a more exciting moment is produced if a dark empty stage has light swelling up on it, instead of two pieces of cloth being drawn apart to reveal a scene. A blackout, done either slowly or quickly at the end of a play, gives the same exciting effect. For arena productions or for theatre-in-the-round, lighting is always used to mark the beginning and the end of a play. Sometimes there is a control which will dim the *house lights* separately from those shining on the stage. This can be a real help, because an audience can be quieted slowly as the lights above the auditorium fade out.

Always remember that the dimmer control must be used with care and sensitivity. A clumsy operator who shoves the dimmer levers on and off instead of easing them gently, can ruin an effect as delicate as a cross fade or a slow blackout.

Be careful when angling lights for arena or in-the-round that there is no overspill to dazzle members of the audience, and lastly, remember that the play and the people in it are more important than the machinery you are using. The lights MUST be the servant of the actors, and it is the lights that must be moved about and changed if an effect is not right, NOT the actors.

SAFETY HINTS

Do not climb a ladder on the stage to work the lights unless the safety of the ladder has been checked and someone is present

49. Angling stage lights. The safest method of getting up to the lights to angle them is on a tower, like the one in the photo. The operator then has both hands free to angle the instruments, which is not the case if he is clinging to a ladder. —*David Richardson, reproduced by permission of Mr. J. K. Wilkinson.*

Stage Lighting

while you are using it. All electrical connections and installations must be checked by a person knowledgeable in the field of electricity.

Water is a conductor of electricity, so do not operate the dimmers or touch the instruments with wet hands, and NEVER, NEVER make your own lights or use homemade lights. If you do not have the sort of equipment that has been mentioned, it is better to do without.

Even without using real light for a play, it is still fun to make a lighting plot with a color design and a cue sheet and to create in theory the atmosphere you think would be the right one. Read a play (or part of one) and see if you have any ideas about how it could be lit. The opening scenes of *Macbeth,* by William Shakespeare, are a good choice with which to experiment.

SOUND EFFECTS

There are two methods of making sound effects. One is to make a prerecorded tape of all the sounds that are needed during a play, and the second is to make the effects "live" while the play is being performed. For both methods you will need a cue sheet similar to the one shown for lighting, indicating exactly where the sound must be made and what it consists of. The cue sheet must also show the length of time that the effect is to be heard together with its volume level. The loudness of a sound effect is dependent not merely on the type of effect, but also the size of the auditorium, so it is necessary to have a friend sitting in the audience during rehearsals to tell you what the effect is like and whether it is too loud or too soft.

Live sound requires some form of machine or instrument from which the sound is produced. Thunder can be made by shaking a piece of thin flexible metal (no less than 1 sq. yard) lightly to produce soft rumblings or vigorously if you want a sharp clap. The sound of rain (or waves on the seashore) can be made by swirling a tambourine round and round with some gravel or small stones in it (illustration 50). The faster you swirl, the heavier will be the sound of the rain falling or the waves pounding the beach. Gunshots should really be made with a

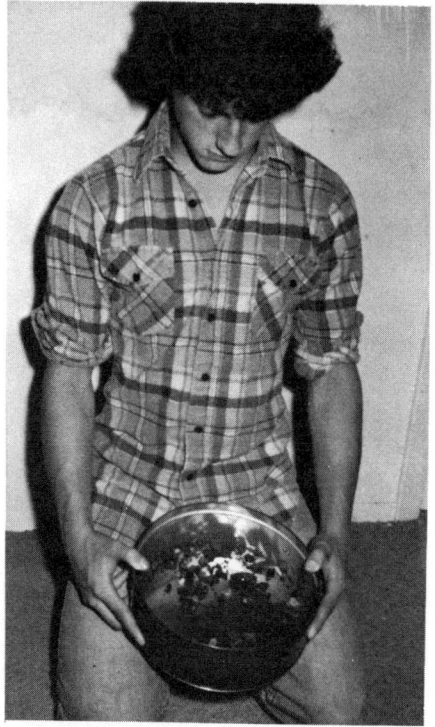

50. Making a rain sound.
—*Photograph by P. Culleton*

sports starting pistol loaded with blank cartridges and fired away from other people, and at arms length. Bursting a paper bag or dropping a stage weight does not have the same ring of truth. Shops that sell musical instruments often have various bird and slide whistles, if you need these sorts of effects, but they can be rather expensive. You will have fun if you experiment with different ways of making the sounds that you need. But live sound does have some disadvantages, because it can seem rather "homemade" and unrealistic. The effect of a crowd, made by having people who are offstage all talking at once, is difficult to control when you want the sound kept to a specific volume level, and the "machinery" and "instruments" you can use do have an unfortunate habit of not responding as

Sound Effects

well as they seemed to during rehearsals. A lot of harm can result if the thunder sheet is dropped while the sound operator is trying to store it out of the way after using it. For a play that has only a few simple effects live sound is ideal, but if there is a long and complicated sound plot it is best to make a pre-recorded tape.

RECORDED SOUND

The tape recorder you will need to use should be the type that takes large spools, called a reel-to-reel machine. Cassette machines cannot be used because you must be able to see the tape clearly. Also reel-to-reel recorders work at faster speeds than cassettes, and a faster speed will give a better quality of sound. If you can plug some extension loudspeakers into the recorder, you will be able to make the sound come from the direction the audience expects (illustration 51).

Make a list of all the sounds that are required in the order that they should be heard, and the length of time each should take, then record the sounds onto the tape in the same order.

51. Tape recorder and loudspeakers positioned for offstage sound. Either one or both of the speakers can be plugged into the tape recorder, depending from which side the sound is meant to be coming.

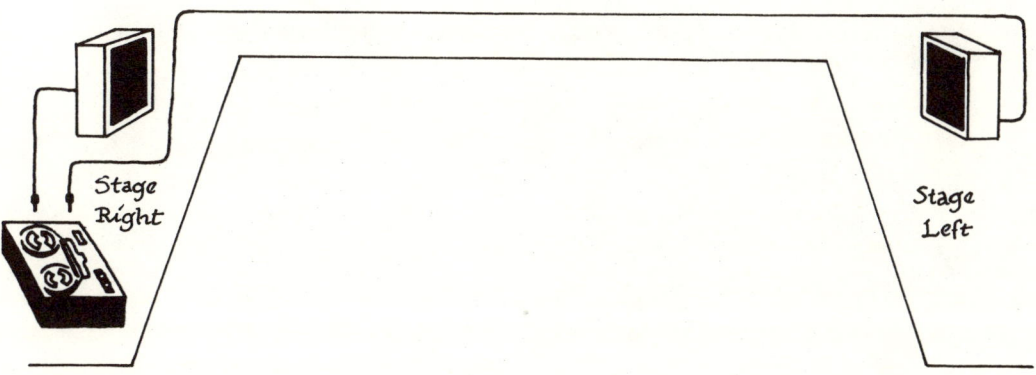

Leave a small gap of unrecorded tape between each effect. Each sound must now be cued accurately so that you know exactly WHEN it is to come, and WHAT it will be. To do this first stick an arrow on the deck of the tape recorder so that it points straight towards the tape. Play the tape from the beginning, until you come to the first sound. Stop the machine and wind the tape back a little to just before the first sound is heard. Write the number of the cue on a piece of white paper and Scotch-tape it onto the tape so that the number is directly in line with the arrow. Both the paper and the Scotch tape must be less than the width of the recording tape. If you are dealing with the first sound effect then that will be cue 1, and you should write 1 on the paper. Repeat this procedure for all the other effects, indicating the start of each one with a cue number. This will take some time to do, but if you are careful and accurate the sound will be easy to operate during a performance. All you have to do is to line up the numbers with the arrow, and when a part of the play comes that requires an effect you merely start the recorder at the moment the sound is needed (illustration 52). Should you find that there is a short

52. Lining up a cue number with the arrow.
   —*David Richardson, reproduced by permission of Mr. J.K. Wilkinson.*

Sound Effects   73

pause before the sound is heard, or that the opening of the sound is "cut" into, then you will have to reposition the number on the tape. If you have timed the amount of sound needed for each cue, there will be no need to mark where the sound should end. When no more sound is needed, either stop the machine, or fade the sound out with the volume control before stopping the machine, and simply wind the tape on until you reach the next cue number. When the tape has been cued in, a cue sheet should be made like the one shown in illustration 53.

Sometimes it is necessary to provide a repetitive effect which must last for a long time, such as a peal of church bells. This problem can be overcome by making a *tape loop*, which is a short length of recording tape long enough to fit around the tape heads and the spools, without being too tight. The loop is made by joining the two ends that have been cut and making as many COMPLETE recordings of the effect that you can get on the loop. To do this you will find it easier if you use a slower tape speed. You should indicate on the loop exactly where the effect begins.

Cue	Type	Speaker	Duration	Volume	Tone		Remarks
					Bass	Treble	
1	Opening Music	Both S.L. & S.R.	35 secs.	6	2	3	Fade in over 5 secs. Fade out over the last 5 secs.
2	Dog Barking	S.R.	15 secs.	8	3	3	Switch on. Switch off when completed.

53. A sound effects cue sheet for use with a sound tape and tape recorder. Not all sound effects can be timed so accurately. Sometimes a separate cue will be needed to indicate when the sound is to stop.

When you make a tape recording, you will automatically erase any sound that was originally on the tape. You can also cut sections out of the tape and either throw them away or reposition them in another part of the recording. This is called *editing,* and most stereo shops sell reasonably inexpensive kits for this purpose. If you do edit your tapes, always make a clean diagonal cut in the tape. The ends should butt together, NOT overlap. The adhesive-backed tape used to join the ends should be stuck on the shiny side of the recording tape, which is the side that does not have the sound on it.

Making a sound-effects tape takes quite a long time—not only do the effects have to be cued accurately, they also have to be recorded onto the tape. Recordings of "live" sounds can be made with a microphone, but it is possible to get most of the sounds you will need off special sound-effects phonograph records. There are a lot of these available, offering a wide selection of effects, and they can be bought from most record shops. Never record a sound effect from a record by using a microphone to pick up the sound from the phonograph speaker, because the sound quality will be poor, and unless you are working in absolute silence, you may record other sounds that have nothing to do with the effect you want. Instead the *output* jack from the phonograph should be linked by a connecting cable to the *input* jack of the tape recorder (sometimes labeled *phono*). You will have to make a few test recordings to see if the jacks are correctly linked, and to check that the recording level is neither too loud nor too soft.

Playing sound effects straight from a phonograph during the performance of a play, is to be discouraged. It is no easy task to try and get exactly the right part of a record that you may need, and anyone backstage could bump into the table which holds the equipment, causing the pickup arm to skate across the record.

Once a sound-effects tape has been made, the giving of the sound cue is a reasonably easy job, but it is vital that whoever operates the tape recorder has plenty of time to practice with it, and to understand thoroughly how to use it.

Sound is rather like light because when it is switched on it is immediately obvious. It should be accurately timed and above all it should add to the atmosphere of the play. As the lighting operator has slider dimmers to alter the intensity of the lights, the sound operator has volume and tone (bass and treble) controls to alter the volume and quality of the sound. Practice in using these controls is as important as knowing how to start and stop the tape, and a high degree of sensitivity is needed to produce good sound effects that are just right. The stop and start mechanism on most machines is inclined to be rather noisy, so every effort should be made to prevent loud clicks coming from the controls at the beginning and the end of a cue.

The end of the last section on stage lighting suggested that you practice by lighting the opening scene of *Macbeth* by William Shakespeare. Try now to apply the sound effects and see if you can get the sound and light to work simultaneously. For the first scene of *Macbeth* you will need an introductory sound—perhaps some weird music—that sets the mood of the scene and secures the audience's attention. As the music slowly fades away, the lights should gradually "grow" on the stage and . . . but it is best if you read the scene and create your own effects.

54. McCarter Theatre production of *A Christmas Carol*.
—*Photograph by Robert I. Faulkner.*

MAKEUP, COSTUME AND WARDROBE

MAKEUP

When actors are performing on stage they are usually working under very bright lights that tend to flatten their faces and drain them of their natural color. Stage makeup is worn to counteract this tendency. It restores color to the face and emphasizes the main features. It is also applied to give the face character—often making the face appear older than it really is, by altering the features. The sort of domestic cosmetic that women use to beautify their faces is not really suitable for stage purposes, because it lacks the strength and variety in color that *grease paint* has. Grease paint is made in sticks of varying size and in a wide range of colors, which can be mixed together to give different shades as required, so that many different types of character can be created. You can obtain stage makeup from any theatrical makeup store. Here is a list of the basic contents of a makeup box. The color names are, by and large, the same for all manufacturers. Liners are the smaller sticks of grease paint.

Grease paint	**Liners**
flesh color	medium blue
yellow/white	medium green
brown	carmine
brick red	lake
white	black

Other Requirements

Tins of powder (neutral for general use, brownish for darker shading, and rose for lighter)
A large fluffy powder puff
A jar of cold cream
A very thin paint brush
An old towel
A box of tissues
A mirror (very necessary if you are going to make yourself up).

Stage makeup is an art form in its own right and too large a subject to be written about in great detail within this book. You can only learn about it and the many effects that it can create by practicing either on your own face or that of a friend. Illustrations 55 and 56 show two of the most common makeups, a straight makeup which emphasizes the natural features of the face, and a character makeup. The grease paint should never be applied too thickly but should be spread lightly and evenly with the finger tips. Whatever you are attempting, there is a standard procedure which should always be followed.

First the face should be thoroughly cleansed by rubbing cold cream into the skin wherever the make up is to be applied. Rub the cream well up into the hairline, on and behind the ears and any part of the neck and chest that will be exposed when the costume is worn. Do not make the face up as if it were a mask and had nothing to do with the rest of the body—a sunburnt face supported by a lily-white neck looks very unconvincing! Take the cold cream off with tissues and then apply a base foundation made with one or several colors mixed together. Rub the foundation in lightly and evenly, so that there are no streaks. Hollows and shadows are put on next, using dark colors. Dab the color on with the middle finger, starting at the center of the hollow and smoothing to the edges. Thin lines should be drawn on with the paint brush. Careful attention

Makeup, Costume and Wardrobe

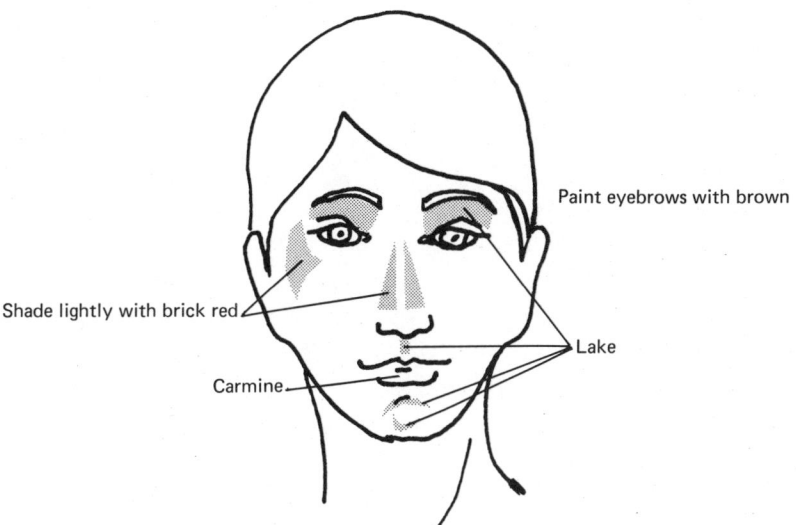

55. A straight makeup. —*S. MacGregor.*

56. A character makeup. All lines and shadows must be smoothed out evenly so that there are no hard edges. —*S. MacGregor.*

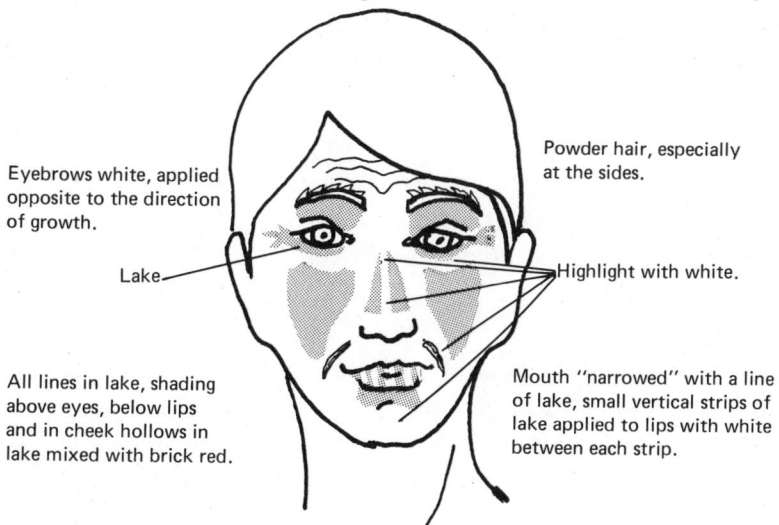

must be given to the eyes, as they are the actor's most expressive feature. All the high points of the face, such as the cheek bones and the middle of the nose should be highlighted with either white or yellow/white. Finally, color and shape the lips. The makeup is completed when it looks even and natural under a strong light. Any lines which are too severe should be smoothed down using the tip of the little finger. Finally, the face is lightly dusted over with powder, which helps to "set" the makeup, and prevents the colors from running or smudging.

All makeup is easily removed by smearing cold cream over the face and wiping it off with tissues.

Beards and moustaches are made by gluing crepe hair to the face. This can be bought in a variety of shades to suit the coloring you want. It should be unraveled and then teased by pulling it gently over the steam from a kettle, taking care not to scald your hands in the steam. The part of the face that is to take the hair should be cleaned of makeup and a small quantity of spirit gum adhesive applied to the cleaned area. The hair is then pressed firmly to it and held under pressure for a few seconds, sticking the ENDS of the crepe hair to the face, so that it appears to grow outwards. Once the hair is firmly positioned, it can be trimmed with a pair of scissors to the shape you require. More hair will have to be stuck on if the beard or moustache is not thick enough. A light tug will remove it painlessly when you have finished with it, and the spirit gum will hold it all together so that it can be reused.

COSTUME

It is not possible to deal with the complexities of costume making within one short chapter, because, like makeup, it is a craft which requires expertise and a thorough knowledge of the techniques used in design, pattern making, sewing, and the use of fabrics. Fashion changes in the history of every country are numerous, and you should consult specialist books on the

Makeup, Costume and Wardrobe

subject of historical costume to see what sort of clothes would be needed in any play you may be helping with.

Once you have decided on the style of clothes needed by the male and female characters in a play, simple drawings can be made and colored. If you feel that you would like to experiment, you could try and adapt old garments into pieces of period costume. Old blankets which are not too highly patterned can be useful as cloaks or outer garments for "rough" characters in period plays. Even discarded curtains and tablecloths are useful as improvised robes. Shoes are often a problem, but again simple improvisations can be quite effective. A character in a medieval play, for example, could wear long socks over the tights they would probably wear, the socks being turned down at the ankle. Naturally they should not have any holes in them, and they should be a plain color.

Should you feel confident enough to want to buy material to create a simple costume, the best material to use is felt, because it can be stitched and glued either to itself or to other fabrics, and when cut to shape does not require hemming as it does not easily fray. Hats, such as the three-cornered types (tricorns), bowlers, and toppers can be made out of a stiff material called buckram. The buckram is cut or bent into a shape, and the shape made permanent by pinning or stapling, then covered with felt which can be sewn or glued on.

Most amateur groups, when performing a play, rent the clothes they need from a theatrical costume house. The cost is met with part of the money gained from the ticket sales.

WARDROBE

When renting costumes, full details of the measurements of each member of the cast should be entered on a chart like the one shown in illustration 57. The head measurements are for hats and wigs, should they be needed. The remarks column should indicate the colors of individual garments and any accessories that the character should have, such as handbags, fans, or swords. The costumer may not be able to supply everything that you ask for, especially where color is concerned. Remember that he has the job of finding garments that will fit the sizes specified, and that is difficult enough.

However, the color and style of costume is most important because it affects other aspects of your stagecraft, most noticeably the lighting and scenery design, and although you may not be the person who does the renting of the costumes, what the people in the play wear will be important to you. Color is important because it will dictate your choice of colors in the lighting plot. Experiment to see what would happen to an orange garment if it were lit with a green color filter in the light. Similarly, a lady wearing a crinoline (a petticoat with hoops sewn in it to expand the skirt) might find it difficult to enter the

Name of Character	Full Height	Chest	Waist	Hips	Inside Arm	Inside Leg	Head Poll to Nape	Circumference	Remarks

57. Measurement chart for renting costumes. Depending on the costumes required, other measurements may have to be given, such as the distance from shoulder to knee.

stage if the door openings were too narrow. So even before a play is rehearsed, and the set and the lighting are thought about, it is first necessary to know what sort of costumes will be worn.

When the costumes have been assembled, there should always be someone whose job it is to care for them, so that they do not become creased or torn. Each complete costume should be checked off against the original list made, and then hung, tied, or pinned to a coat hanger. A label is tied to each hanger indicating who the costume is for, and what it all consists of. Changes of costume are labeled in the same way. The actors should be encouraged to replace their costumes on the hangers immediately after use.

Wardrobe care must include the washing, drying, and ironing of those pieces that become easily soiled, such as shirts, tights, and socks. The bigger garments may need pressing to remove the creases, and a steam iron is useful for this, but if one is not available then a dry iron can be used, as long as there is a damp cloth between the garment and the iron. Always check on the suitability of the materials before any washing or ironing is done, as some materials are easily damaged.

Try and find a play or part of a play in which you can persuade friends to take part and improvise costumes for it. If you can design a simple set with a lighting and sound-effects plot so much the better. By rehearsing a scene you will begin to learn how the many aspects of stagecraft fit together to make a performance.

If you cannot decide on a play, try something out of *Macbeth* again, but this time work on Act 1 scene 3. Shakespeare is ideal because you can create many different effects to enhance the script. The stage directions are not his, but the work of later editors and actors practicing their own stagecraft, so read the text with some friends and form your own ideas about how to interpret the words in the play.

BACKSTAGE ORGANIZATION

So far this book has dealt with all the separate "departments" that are used in stagecraft. All of them—lighting, sound, props, wardrobe—have one task in common: to help establish and maintain the atmosphere of the play for which they are being used. Each department, responsible for creating different effects, is thoroughly organized within itself, and will be made up of a small group of people working as a team. But there may be other jobs to do: switching the auditorium lights on and off, opening and closing the curtains (if they are being used), and resetting the scenery and furniture. This will require additional stage crew, called *ASM'S (assistant stage managers)*, who, like everybody else, will require plenty of time to practice their jobs. The opening and closing of curtains needs as much care as the fading of sound or light. The resetting of scenery and furniture must be carefully organized and rehearsed, whether it is done behind closed curtains or in full view of the audience. In addition, there are two other jobs which must be done backstage: *calling* and *stage managing*.

The call boy has the task of warning the cast when they will be needed on stage, and it is best to get the actors ready for their entrances about ten minutes before they are due to appear. There are good reasons for this. First, it lessens the chances of an actor being late for an entry onto the stage, and second, it means that only those who are needed remain in the wings, which is especially important if you are working on a small proscenium stage with little wing space. Actors tend to get excited and noisy, and they are best kept away from the stage until they are needed. A lot of noise coming from offstage can be very harmful to a performance.

In the professional theater the *stage manager* has the job of "cueing in" effects departments such as lighting and sound, which have to produce their effects at a given moment during the course of a play. For this, a stage manager's desk is needed, together with two or three cue lights. The components for this piece of equipment can be quite costly, and the whole thing can take a long time to make and install, but if you can make one, you will get a lot of satisfaction in being able to cue lighting and sound effects with great accuracy, and in so doing you will be controlling the running of the whole show. Illustration 58 is a simplified wiring diagram of the cue system, which is electrically safe, but ON NO ACCOUNT should it be connected to an electrical outlet. The car battery will give an adequate amount of power, provided that it is periodically charged on a battery charger and the cells are topped up with distilled water.

The system works by first installing a cue light in a prominent place. You can have as many cue lights as you have "departments" that need cueing, although it will probably be necessary to have only three: one by the stage lighting control, another situated where the sound effects are to be operated, and one placed by the switches that control the auditorium lights.

The cue light is made of a box containing two bulb holders and bulbs, which should have a slightly lower voltage rating than the battery which supplies the power, because if several are switched on at once the bulbs will glow less brightly. The box should be divided into two compartments, with red color

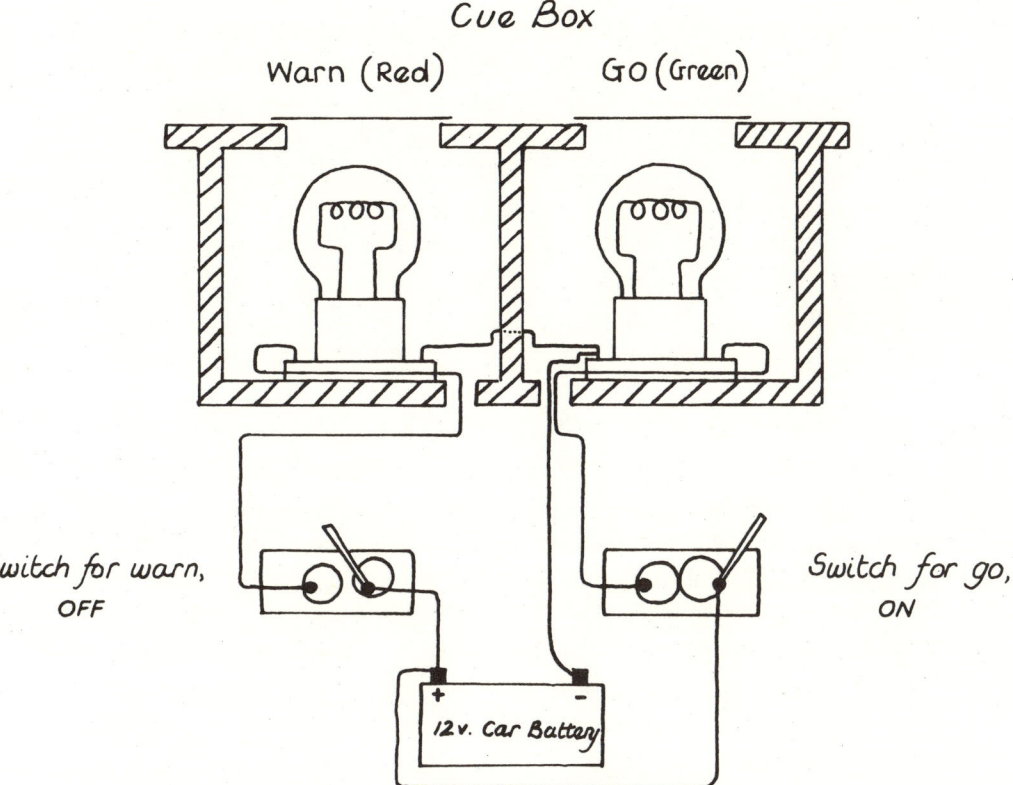

58. Wiring diagram for a cue signaling system.

medium stuck over one and green over the other. The switches on the stage manager's desk must operate the red and green (warn and go) cue lights independently. The red cue light is switched on by the stage manager about 30 seconds before the actual cue has to be made. This warns the operators that a cue is imminent, and gives them time to prepare themselves for the effect that is detailed on their individual cue sheets. As soon as the exact moment arrives for that cue to start, the stage manager signals the "department" concerned by switching on the green light, and the effect begins at precisely that very moment. Both cue lights should then be switched off until the next cue needs to be given.

The beauty of this system is that only one person—the stage manager—needs to follow the play script as the actors go through it. It is very difficult for effects operators to follow the script, read the cue sheet, and carry out the effects; and there is always the possibility that they may miss a cue, or, if tucked away at the back of the stage, be unable to hear the actors clearly. The stage manager essentially has to hear the play and follow it, so it is far easier, and makes for much greater accuracy if the effects operators can take their cues from a signaling system that warns them when to get ready, and tells them exactly when to do each cue. This method will also be useful if there is a need to have several things (lights, sound, and curtains) all operated simultaneously. The exact moment for giving the warn and go cues must be decided upon during rehearsals, and should be entered into the *stage manager's copy* as shown in illustration 59. It is easy to read if the lines indicating the cues are color-coded—red for warn and green for go. The vertical lines drawn in the columns, from the moment that the warn light is switched on, should stop when the light is switched off.

The stage manager's copy is an important document and should be kept safely when not in use. It contains all the necessary information for the technical running of a play, and is made by dismantling a copy of the play script and clipping the leaves into a loose-leaf binder, alternating each leaf with a blank sheet of paper on which are drawn the columns. The information that each column contains is written in pencil first, in case there are any alterations to be made as rehearsals progress, and inked in when all the information is finally decided. The moves column contains the important moves of the actors, and this means that the stage manager should attend every rehearsal in

Moves	Effects	Misc.	Electrics			
		3 witches ready to enter			"MACBETH"	
1: Three witches enter from S.L. to D.S. edge of rostrum 'B' as thunder is heard. Take up positions. x 1st x x 2nd. 3rd.	Warn Cue 1 Go Cue 1 Thunder (for 5 secs.)		Warn Cue 1 Go Cue 1		Act I. Scene iii.	
				CHARACTERS:	First WITCH, Second WITCH, Third WITCH, MACBETH, BANQUO.	
				SCENE:	A Heath. Thunder. Enter the three Witches.	
				1 WITCH:	Where hast thou been, sister?	
				2 WITCH:	Killing swine.	
				3 WITCH:	Sister, where thou?	
2: 1st witch leans over towards 2nd. and 3rd. who huddle closer towards rostrum.		Macbeth and Banquo ready to enter.		1 WITCH: 2	A sailor's wife had chestnuts in her lap. And mounch'd, and mounch'd, and mounch'd: "Give me". quoth I:— "Aroint thee, witch!" the rump-fed ronyon cries. Her husband's to Aleppo gone, master o' the Tiger:	
3: 2nd. and 3rd. witch move D.S.					But in a sieve I'll thither sail, And like a rat without a tail; I'll do, I'll do, and I'll do.	
				2 WITCH:	I'll give thee a wind.	
				1 WITCH:	Thou art kind.	
				3 WITCH:	And I another.	
4: 1st witch u.stage, slightly, straightening				1 WITCH:	I myself have all the other; And the very ports they blow, All the quarters that they know I' the shipman's card. I'll drain him dry as hay: Sleep shall neither night nor day Hang upon his penthouse lid; He shall live a man forbid. Weary sev'n-nights, nine times nine,	
5: 2nd. witch up onto rostrum 'B' edge to R. of 1st witch. 3rd witch faces 1st. Witch.	Warn Cue 2			3	Shall he dwindle, peak, and pine: Though his bark cannot be lost, Yet it shall be tempest-tost.	
6: 3rd witch, straightening up moves onto rostrum 'B' to D.L. of 1st witch.	Cue 2 Go 2 Side Drum	Warn Cue 2		4	Look what I have.	
				2 WITCH: 5	Show me, show me.	
		Ross and Angus ready to enter.		1 WITCH:	Here I have a pilot's thumb,	
				6	Wrack'd, as homeward he did come.	
				3 WITCH:	A drum! a drum!	
7: 3 witches join hands and circle.				7	Macbeth doth come.	
				ALL:	The weird sisters, hand in hand, Posters of the sea and land, Thus do go about, about:	
	Warn Cue 3			1 WITCH:	Thrice to thine,	
				2 WITCH:	And thrice to mine,	
8: Witches stop circling and finish. 3 2 1				3 WITCH: 8	And thrice again,	
	Cue Go 3 Side Drum Stop.		Go Cue 2	ALL:	To make up nine.	
				1 WITCH:	Peace! — the charm's wound up.	

59. Part of a stage manager's copy.

order to write them down. The miscellaneous column should contain the names of the actors who have to be called, together with changes in set and props, and the order in which these changes are made. Cues for house lights and curtains can go in this column too. The stage copy is usually made up by the stage manager, who fills in the appropriate information.

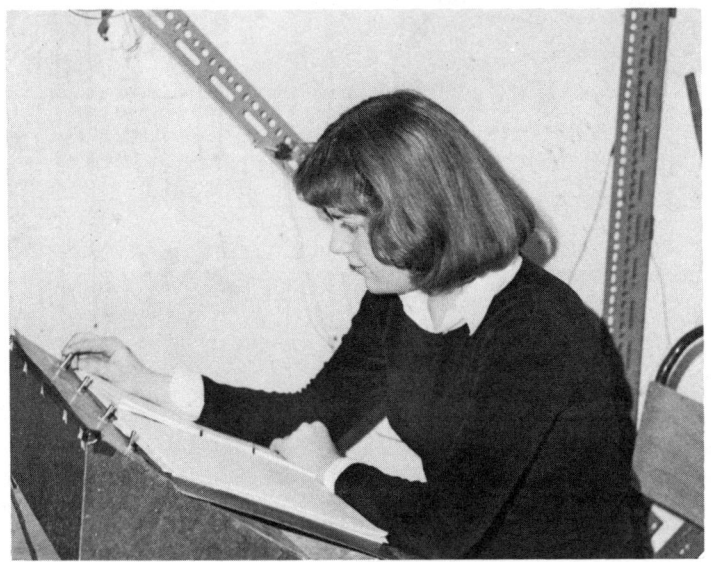

60. The stage manager at the stage manager's desk.
—*David Richardson, reproduced by permission of Mr. J. K. Wilkinson.*

The stage manager is one of the most important people backstage, during both rehearsals and performance. It is his job to weld all the ASMs and stage crew into one efficient team who will work together for the good of the play. He must even make sure that the actors are part of that team. A good stage manager will be able to undertake any of the technical work that has to be done on the stage: to help the crew and make sure that they all have enough time to practice their tasks quietly and accurately. He must also be prepared to make quick decisions if anything goes wrong during a performance. But although he is in charge backstage, he should be humble enough to sweep the stage clean before a performance—if there is no one else to do it!

Should you find yourself helping backstage during a play, it is hoped that you may find some of the information in this book helpful for the job that you have to do. Most of the ordinary materials and equipment you will need will be obtainable from suppliers in your own area. For more complicated items such as materials and paint for scenery, or stage-lighting equipment, you will need to contact specialist firms who can supply you with catalogs and price lists. The most useful addresses for you to know are:

Associated Theatrical Designers Ltd.
145 W. 71st Street
New York, NY 10023

Make Up Center Ltd.
150 W. 55th Street
New York, NY 10019

For stage lighting and "heavy" equipment such as stage weights and braces, stands, blocks, etc., contact either of the following:

Times Square Theatrical & Studio Supply
318 W. 47th Street
New York, NY 10036

Gossard & Associates, Inc.
801 E. 134th Street
Bronx, NY 10454

Index

A
Actors, 7, 18, 25, 30, 44, 46, 49, 53, 57-58, 61, 65-66, 77, 83, 85-86, 88, 90
Arena stages, *3*, 9, 15, 22-23, 56, 65-66
  lighting of, 56, 62
Assistant stage manager (ASM), 85, 90
Atmosphere, of a play, 25, 29-30, 53, 57-58, 67, 75, 85
Audience, 7-9, 11-12, 18-23, 25, 31, 59, 65-66, 69

B
Backstage, 25, 59
Beards, 80
Bird sounds, 70
Blackouts, 62, 65-66
Book flats, 39
Box sets, 26, 31

C
Calling, 85-86
Candle props, 49, 51, 52

Cast, the, 18, 25, 27
Castle of Perseverance, The, 7, *9*
Colored lighting, 18, 57-58, 82
Costumes, 25, 80-83
  accessories, 82
  care of, 83
  historical, 81
  how to make, 81
  measuring for, 81-82
  renting of, 81-82
  See also Wardrobe
Cross fades, 62-63, 66
Crowd sounds, 70
Cue lights, 86-88
Cue sheets, 65, 67, 69, 87-88
Cue systems, 86-88, 90
Curtains, 7, 9, 18, 22, 85
Cyclorama (cyc), 18-19, 29, 56, 63

D
Dimmers, 62, 65-67, 75
Door flats, 36, *37*

E
Effects operators, 71, 75, 88

Electrics operator, 61, 65-66
Elizabethan stages, *10,* 23
England, 7, 9
Epidaurus, Greece, theater at, *8*

F
Fireplace flat, 36-38
Fireproofing, 35, 38
Flats, 18, 22, 26, 29, 31
　how to make, 31-39, *40*
　See also Scenery
Floodlights, 54, *56*, 59, 63
Food props, 49
Furniture, 23, 25, 29, 43-44, 85
　See also Props

G
Gilbert and Sullivan, 27
Grease paint. *See* Makeup
Greek theater, 7, *8, 12*
Ground plans, 18-23, 27, 29, 43, 46
Gunshot sounds, 69-70

H
Hair, 80
Hats, 81
Helmets, 47-48
House lights, 65

I
In-the-round stages, 7-9, 15, 22-23, 31, 65-66
　ground plan of, 23
　lighting of, 56, 62

J
Jewelry, 48

L
Lantern props, 49-51
Lighting control, types of, 61-66
Lighting cue sheet, 64-65
Lighting equipment, 15, 53-54, 56-57, 59, 61
Lighting operator, 75
Lighting plot, 58-59, *60*, 64, 67
Lighting techniques, 57-59, 61-64
Lights, placement of, 56-58, 61, 65-66
Live sound, 70-71
Loudspeakers, 71

M
Macbeth, 67, 75, 83
Makeup, 77-78, *79*, 80
Masking flats, 29-30, 38
McCarter Theatre, 17, 76
Moustaches, 80

N
New Jersey Shakespeare Festival, *16*

P
Painting, 38, 41, 43
Parchment, 47
Period plays, 43
Pillars, 39, 41
Plain flats, 38
Playwright, 25
Producer, 25
Props, 25, 29, 44, 46
　how to make, 39, *41*, 46-48
　painting of, 48-49, 51
Props master, 46, *47,*
Props plot, 46
Proscenium arch stages, 12, 15, 17-19, 22-23, 30, 46, 56, 59, 63, 86
　ground plan of, 18-23
　lighting of, 59, 61, 63
　set design for, *45*

Index

R

Rain sounds, 69, *70*
Recorded sound, 71-74
Rehearsals, 65, 88, 90
Rookery Nook, 26, 59
 ground plan of, 26-27
Royalty Theatre, 11

S

Safety hints, 35, 38, 46, 49
Scenery, 11-12, 19-20, 22, 25-26, 29, 43, 85
 building of, 31-35, 39
 designing of, 7, 31
 painting of, 38, 41, 43
 See also Flats
Script, 88-90
Set design, 25-26, 30, 38, 42, 44-45, 59
Shakespeare, William, 67, 75, 83
Shields, 48-49
Sight lines, 19-23, 29
Sound effects, 69-74
 See also Recorded sound; Tape recording sounds
Sound effects cue sheets, 69, 72-73
Sound operator, 71, 75
Spotlights, 53-54, *55*, 57-59, 62

Stage, defined, 23
 dimensions of, 19, 21, 23, 29
 parts of, 18, 21-22, 25, 29, 36, 46
 types of, 7-9, 11-13, 15
Stage crew, 15, 17, 29, 44, 85, 90
Stage directions, 25, 83
Stage-lighting firms, 57, 91
Stage manager, 85-88, 90-91
Swords, 48

T

Tape recording sounds, 71-75
Theater, history of, 7-9, 11-12
Theatrical specialty firms, 91
Thunder sounds, 69, 71
Travers, Ben, *26*
Trees, 39

V

Victoria Theatre, 16

W

Wardrobe. *See* Costumes
Wave sounds, 69
Window flats, 35, *36*

Y

Yeomen of the Guard, The, 27
 ground plan for, *28*, 29
 set design for, 27, *28*